"Michelle Davis's bool :h, prayer, and miracles. d takes you through one family's epoch of unbelievable stress and deep worry for their beloved Nathan. His survival was nothing short of miraculous. As one who participated in his care, I was deeply touched by their sincere and humble faith. Throughout his hospitalization and rehabilitation, they never lost their focus on bringing Nathan before God's throne of grace. Michelle chronicles the story in a way that makes you feel like you were there. I was blessed by my participation in Nathan's care; you will be blessed by reading this book when you see the power of prayer unfold before your eyes."

—Carlos H. Rodriguez, MD, FACS
Chief of Surgical Specialties
Spectrum Health Medical Group
Grand Rapids, Michigan

"Finding Hope on Vegas is a vivid narrative no parent wants to read. Michelle Davis's very personal account of how her faith sustained her while suffering through a severe tragedy involving her oldest son will make every parent contemplate whether their faith is strong enough to withstand something similar. Her book makes one thing crystal clear—God is sovereign, loving, and in complete control of our lives regardless the outcome."

—David and Marilyn Schubert
Coaches for Kairos Speech and Debate Club

"This is a moving account of the power of faith and wonders of modern medicine. For Nate, it clearly took a village to save and restore his young life. Stories like this one give focus, meaning, and purpose to our hundreds of volunteer blood donors and blood bank employees who can be proud of the role they played in Nate's survival and remarkable recovery."

—Carleen Crawford
Director of Community Relations and Marketing
Michigan Blo

"*Finding Hope on Vegas* is a powerfully true story that shook many of us to our core. All of my clinical training coupled with two and a half decades of practice in healthcare were of so little value during those first few days. Any knowledge or skills I possessed seemed to only be a curse, brutally reminding me of the frailty of human life and the near non-existent power man has to preserve it. As I now tearfully reminisce about this horrifying experience, I cannot help but focus on two inescapable truths: (1) how much I adore these dear friends and (2) how gracious God was to Nate Davis and the rest of us that summer. Perhaps Michelle's meticulous efforts to preserve this account will cause you to recognize the beauty in her desperation and surrender . . . and her faith. It is not because of medicine's heroics, however, that he was spared. It was only because the creator of the universe was rich in mercy, displayed great love, and very gracious in saving Nate. My most sincere hope is that you'll read this story and join me in thanking God one more time for his mercy, his love, and his grace so prominently on display throughout this adventure."

— Dr. Jeffrey A. Bates, PharmD, BCGP, FMPA
Associate Dean and Associate Professor
Cedarville University School of Pharmacy
Cedarville, OH

"Faith is tested when tragedy strikes. How we respond is a culmination of how we have lived our faith up to that moment. Michelle shares her family's faith in God when they are staring at the loss of a child and how God responds back to them. If you have ever wondered if saying a prayer has any effect, you need to read this story."

—Mark Graveline
Coordinator of Youth Ministry
Catholic Diocese of Saginaw
Saginaw, MI

FINDING HOPE ON VEGAS

FINDING HOPE ON
VEGAS

a memoir

MICHELLE DAVIS

BookBound Media, LLC
www.bookboundmedia.com

ISBN-13: 978-0-9989652-0-8 (trade paper)
ISBN-10: 0-9989652-0-0 (trade paper)
eISBN-13: 978-0-9989652-1-5 (ePub)
eISBN-10: 0-9989652-1-9 (ePub)

© 2017 Michelle Davis

Publisher: BookBound Media, LLC

Cover Photo: © Candy (Debora) Dzenk
Cover Design: Tonya Woodworth
Interior Design and Formatting: Tonya Woodworth
Photo of Michelle Davis by Gwen McCulloch, Lime Light Studios

To our heavenly father, the creator of life.
To all those who work relentlessly to save and protect life.
To Nathan, who helped me recognize life's precious moments.
To Tim, Danielle, Nathan, Nicholas, Mathew, and Andrew;
you are my purpose and life.

I plead with you—never, ever give up on hope, never doubt, never tire, and never become discouraged. Be not afraid.

—*Saint John Paul II*

CONTENTS

FOREWORD

As I expect the reader will gather, although Nathan's very life hung in the balance, his journey perhaps affected the lives of those around him more than it may have impacted Nathan himself. Having had the pleasure of visiting with him after a nearly full recovery, I know this is true for me. Although I am competitive by nature, I do not see my competitiveness as one-upsmanship on my part. Nor is it the wisdom that inevitably accompanies the ceaseless advance of time. Nathan, although young, is not particularly naïve, nor is he blindly optimistic. I gather that he has a deep, inherent comprehension that he was close to death. Though he was characteristically reserved when discussing it, I could see in his eyes that he knew. With time, his demeanor changed. Anxiousness became acceptance; worry became hope.

I have been wonderfully blessed in a profession that allows me to assist, to comfort, and to ameliorate suffering. At times I have taken it for granted; on other occasions, I have been narcissistically vainglorious about an operative success. Egocentric attitudes like these can derail the most competent physician. Nathan's tragedy emphatically reminds me that usually it is not about us. I work with incredibly talented and gifted individuals, each one part of a large, complex team. We did not "fix" Nathan; I couldn't stop his bleeding. We utilized our knowledge and tools and were deeply committed to and invested in saving him. In these situations, some patients survive. I can't tell you with certainty why some patients like Nathan survive and some don't.

To focus too intently on the medical details, though, is to miss the point. Every one of us faces our mortality; there is but one recorded exception in history. The mystery, beyond our understanding of life, of death, and of life after death is what makes Nathan's experience so compelling. What is our purpose in this life? Why is there suffering? What is the point of it all? As a bit player and a witness to these events, I can say that I could palpably discern what unwavering faith felt like when I interacted with Nathan's family. I, for one, believe it made a difference.

I am truly honored to have been one of many who were able to interact with Nathan and his large devoted family throughout their ordeal. They touched many in profound ways, and I for one am better for having had the privilege. I have asked Nathan more than once what this experience means for him going forward. Refreshingly, he has not given me an answer, certainly not one that is canned or pat. Frankly, it is his and his alone. I, selfishly, have viewed this as a "second chance" for him, one he "should not waste." Perhaps I should take my own advice. We are not blessed with insight of this type every day.

—Dr. Dan Robertson, MD

ACKNOWLEDGMENTS

First, I want to thank the love of my life, Tim! You have always been the source of optimism and strength during the ups and downs of life. During this excruciating experience, these qualities became a beacon for me. You became the rock that kept our disheartened family strong.

Next, I wish to thank my family for all their patience and support over the last year and half as I spent hours writing and rewriting the story.

I wish to recognize the foundational role my parents—Richard and Kathy Cassiday—and my in-laws—Allan and Judi Davis—played throughout this story. Their life-long witness of love, faith, and commitment prepared Tim and me to face the biggest challenge in our lives thus far.

I would like to thank all of our extended family, friends, and strangers that reached out to us. Your love, prayers, and support made a huge difference.

I am forever grateful to Nathan's friends—Dean and Kyle Schunk, Katie Hedrick, Devon Poet, Alicia Ramirez, Cody Cripps, Kennedy Shea, Matt Badger, and Mike McGuire— as well as his cousins Brooke Cassiday and Andrea Newman for visiting us in the hospital the night of the accident and staying with us during those difficult first forty-eight hours.

My acknowledgment would not be complete without

recognizing Dr. Dan Robertson. Not only has he become a hero to my family but his commitment to his profession gives hope to so many facing tragedies. His faith in God appears to drive him forward during bleak moments that emphasize the importance of life. I am also indebted to him for the eloquent foreword, not to mention all of the correspondence over the last year as he advised me medically while writing.

Although I cannot possibly list everyone who was involved, I would like to thank Dr. Carlos Rodriguez, Dr. Amy Spencer, Dr. Jennifer Fromm, Dr. Jeffrey Bonacci, Brad Doepker, and all of the other fantastic medical personnel who gave their all to save Nathan.

It is essential that I recognize the relentless persistence of Danielle and my mom, as they encouraged me to *do something* with my post-traumatic stress journal. It was their drive that brought this faith story to fruition. Also, thanks to Susan Zelt and Pastor John Devries, who casually planted this seed while Nate was recovering.

I would like to thank Kirsten Fortier, a key contributor to the development of this book. Her patience, generosity, and friendship helped me develop my ideas more completely and encouraged me to keep going when I convinced myself the story was not worthy of publication.

A huge thanks to the very talented Tonya Woodworth from BookBound Media, whose expertise, coaching, and commitment has made this book a reality. I appreciate her patience and time especially when fielding all of the late night e-mails, texts, and conversations that pushed me through this daunting process.

Finally, and most importantly, I would like to thank Jesus's mother, Mary, for all her intercessory prayers, and the Holy Spirit who perfectly orchestrated the events surrounding Nate's accident.

PREFACE

I must confess that although our family unexpectedly served as an instrument of God's grace, we are not and never will be a perfect family. Each of us journey toward God in our own way; we continuously succeed and fail. It is only through his grace that any of us can be worthy of his blessings. I feel the need to stress this point before I share the following story.

What started out as a few notes for Nate to grasp the events that transpired during the first forty-eight hours after his accident has spiraled into quite a lengthy summary, especially for someone like me since I am not a writer by nature. Although this book may not perfectly describe all of the details (or all of the people involved for that matter), it is a fairly accurate account of an incredible journey.

Against all odds, Nathan lived! To this day, I cannot truly comprehend how close he was to dying, and Dr. Robertson cemented this reality for me on Nate's last visit when he told me, "I gave him less than a five percent chance to make it through the night!"

While Nate was in the hospital, my family's lives came to a major standstill. Far too many coincidences emerged during those twenty-eight days to not recognize God's hand. As Brad, the on-site paramedic, would later explain to me, "Things just don't fall in line like that, *ever!*"

Because these events were so profound and perfectly orchestrated, I have compiled a summary of them into a separate list at the end of the book, which I have titled "God Moments." Although our family immediately recognized the divine intervention on that fateful day, it was not until I compiled the list that we fully understood the story's scope. It might be worth noting here that some of the information included in that section is not in the story.

With this in mind, our family wishes to share this story of coincidences for many reasons:

- *To give glory to God* for all of the blessings he bestows on us

- *To emphasize the value of life* through the continuous efforts of so many who did not quit even when Nate's situation looked impossible

- *To show how the hand of God works* in all of our lives even when we do not realize it

- *To remind people to surrender* every circumstance to the power of God and ask for the grace to accept the outcome even if it seems to be against our own plan

- *To recognize the power of intercessory prayer* not only from those here on earth, but especially from those in heaven

- *To offer hope* amid chaos and encourage Christians to make a difference in the world through prayer

I am well aware of the fact that God appears to answer so many prayers in this world with a resounding, "No!" This answer can be an agonizing burden. My heart truly goes out to the people who endure such an answer. Over the last year, I have witnessed with a heavy heart the noes to numerous prayers for healing of friends and family, and

I have had to attend many funerals.

Overwhelmed with waves of great despair, we feared the outcome to our desperate pleas for God to spare Nathan's life would also result in a "no" several times throughout our family's journey. Yet, in these moments of weakness, and through a tremendous outpouring of prayer, we discovered a profound gift: hope.

Up until then, *hope* was an elusive concept that I just could not quite understand. Merriam-Webster defines hope as a "desire with expectation of obtainment" or "to expect with confidence."[1] G.K. Chesterton beautifully defined it this way: "Hope is the power of being cheerful in circumstances which we know to be desperate."[2] Probably the best description of hope for me was from a friend who is a priest. He explained that hope comes to us when we understand that our daily challenges, whether great or small, are not only intimately known by God but also specifically allowed by God to help us journey toward heaven.

It was through this journey that I came to truly understand this explanation of hope. The power of this one word imparted peace upon my family, something I never imagined was possible, especially during some of our bleakest moments. The fruits of everyone's prayers were not only seen by the sparing of Nate's life but also felt through the hope and peace that surrounded us. Hope gave our family the means to cope in the face of this terrible tragedy.

Even though they were some of the most difficult moments of my life thus far, I personally never want to forget the events that transpired on August 9, 2014. They brought out the best in so many people: my husband, kids, extended families, doctors, nurses, churches, and communities. I want this experience to continue to bring out the best in me, too. I expect, with confidence, to be more appreciative, helpful,

---

1. https://www.merriam-webster.com/dictionary/hope
2. www/goodreads.com/quotes/tag/cheerful

and compassionate to other people on their life's journey as so many people were to us. I cannot thank enough those who saved Nate's life or prayed for our family. I do, however, try to thank God for these generous souls every day. Someone once told me that the only way to thank everyone is by making a difference in someone else's life. Sometimes that difference can be a simple prayer or appeal to God on their behalf. That, my friends, is what I believe we are called to do as Christians!

May God bless all prayer warriors, for their humble job silently, yet profoundly, impacts the world. These simple efforts, combined with God's abundant grace, are truly the foundation of finding hope in what can be a hopeless world for so many people. Amen!

INTRODUCTION

I t was a beautiful Saturday afternoon in May when the Davis and Cassiday families gathered together at some property owned by my parents, Richard and Kathy Cassiday, to prepare for yet another event. The property itself was nothing special. It consisted of thirty-nine partially wooded acres with trails that provided hours of dirt bike entertainment for the thirteen Davis and Cassiday cousins. Three towering maple trees stood over a large field. Providing some shade, it was the perfect spot to set up base camp and a fire pit. For years, running water was the only luxury we had, thanks to a couple of gas generators. Earlier that spring, we finally finished construction on a small pole barn that we had started the previous summer. It became the camp kitchen: complete with a propane stove, sink, and food prep area. The kitchen area had been cleaned and restocked earlier in the day to prepare for the summer. Memorial Day weekend, the official start to the camping season, was just a week away, and we were anticipating a slew of campers as we tried to get everything in order.

Gatherings like this were typical for such a crowd since we were such a close-knit family. When there was work to be done, we all pitched in to help. As the ladies worked in the kitchen area, the rest of the gang spent the day working hard: mowing the large camping area, setting up horseshoe pits, erecting a temporary pool, and painting picnic tables and the wooden playground. We knew the hard work would pay off the following Saturday for the huge celebration we had planned.

This property had become hallowed ground in a sense to my three brothers—Bryan, Jason, and Steve—and me, since our families and many great friends camped here throughout the summer. It provided a fun escape for the kids and the adults, to halt the craziness in all of our lives, even if it was used only a few weekends during the summer.

The venture began one Labor Day weekend over thirteen years ago when my sister-in-law Kelli and I decided to camp there. Our oldest kids were still quite small, so we chose the spot since it was fairly close to home. It was only natural for this hallowed ground to become the location for their dual graduation party.

Nevertheless, this day was vastly different than anyone could have expected nine months earlier. A lot had changed for everyone since August. Gratitude filled the air while everyone worked together cheerfully. We were all very thankful to have two graduates for the dual graduation party next weekend rather than just one.

After a long day's work, the grill was loaded with barbecued chicken to feed the hungry crowd. When dinner was finally ready, one of the grandkids rang the large cast-iron dinner bell. Everyone instinctively gathered in a huge circle and held hands to say the blessing before we ate. My father, after all of the difficult times our family had been through, became a little sentimental and asked, "Please, would everyone please say something they are thankful for before we eat?" Everyone was a little surprised. This was a Thanksgiving tradition and not expected at a graduation, but, again, this was no ordinary gathering.

As I listened to a few of the twenty-three family members

express their thanks, I became lost in my own thoughts. *What am I thankful for? Where could I begin? The last nine months had been such a roller coaster for all of us! What should I say?* There were too many things to be thankful for: my husband (Tim), the kids, love, family, God, hope! How could I choose just one?

Chapter 1

The Family

My child, when you come to serve the Lord,
prepare yourself for trials.[1]

It was Saturday, August 9, 2014. What started as a warm, typical summer Saturday swiftly turned into a day I would never forget! Up until then, I had not personally experienced a traumatic event in my family circle. This day would not only drastically challenge my faith but also change my perspective on family, friends, and life forever.

Tim and I were high school sweethearts from rival schools. We met on a blind date, thanks to my best friend, Michelle Gerow-Ellis, who introduced us. After dating for almost six years, we finally married on December 29, 1990. Majoring in computer science, I finished college at Central Michigan University that spring. Right after graduation, I landed a computer engineering position with Zenith Data Systems, a pioneer in the very young computer industry.

1. Sirach 2:1 New American Bible, Revised Edition (NABRE)

Tim had attended college at Michigan Technological University in the Upper Peninsula for a couple of years before we were married. After his sophomore year, he decided to change direction and accepted a job with Michigan Bell Telephone Company. This suited him better, since he did not like the confines of a classroom. Two years into college made him realize that he needed a job outdoors, where he could physically move around. He did not wish to be stuck in an office position, even as an engineer. It turned out to be a great position with excellent benefits, and when I started working in St. Joseph, Michigan, shortly after college, a job became available for him to transfer.

Shortly after his transfer, Tim and I purchased a fixer-upper. Four years later Danielle—or Dani as we affectionately called her—was born. Our whole world changed! We were no longer the Dual Income, No Kids (DINK) couple doing whatever we wanted, whenever we wanted.

The transition to parenthood went fairly smoothly as Danielle proved to be an easy child. When Tim and I brought her home from the hospital, she slept through the night without making a fuss. She was inquisitive and could learn almost anything very quickly. As such, she started talking relatively early, and she always seemed to know what she wanted. Danielle could usually figure out how to get it, too. Even at two years old, this very independent attitude would sometimes get her into trouble, especially when she would forgo naptime at day care. She was too antsy and had trouble keeping quiet while all the other toddlers slept. As she grew, I began to admire her energy, determination, creativity, and overall enthusiasm, which would brighten anyone's day.

Tim and I loved our new roles as parents and, as expected, everything continued to change. We had just gotten the hang of having one child when God blessed us with another just two-and-a-half years later. While I was pregnant with Nathan, my job became unstable, so Tim convinced me to stay home. I thought that was a crazy suggestion, since I had worked so hard to earn a degree. I slowly warmed up to the idea, however, especially since both of us were raised by stay-at-home moms.

That was when I met Darla Nickels. She was expecting her third child when she came up to me in church and boldly introduced herself one Sunday afternoon. Since I was a little reserved because I did not know many people at the parish, Darla's fearless approach intimidated me at first. As she continued to engage in conversation, I soon found her to be very friendly and endearing. Just before we finished talking, she told me that a few of the moms from the parish would get together during the week. She invited me to join their little group. I did, and made wonderful friendships with a great group of homeschooling moms.

Darla was the unofficial ringleader. I could tell right away that she was very passionate about her beliefs. Already a seasoned mom, she continuously challenged the rest of us to grow in our faith. She always had a new prayer, rosary, or parenting book to share with us. Darla constantly encouraged us with cute little lessons about Jesus that we could share with our children to help them come to know him too. Through her constant joy and enthusiasm for God, Darla inspired me to live my faith, not to just show up to church for an hour on Sunday to fulfill my obligation. She was quite a mentor, too. She truly lived the gospels of Christ in many ways: through her selfless acts of kindness, financial support for those in need, constant prayers for others, etc.

Thanks to Darla, I had an unquenchable desire to dive deeper into the Catholic faith. I read every doctrinal book I could get my hands on, attended bible studies, and tried to attend daily Mass.

It was not long before Tim warned me, "If you keep going to church every day, you're going to be known as one of those crazy church ladies."

After meeting Darla, seeking the confessional was common for me. Once I had rediscovered my faith, I tried to receive the sacrament of reconciliation often, usually at our parish in Sanford, Michigan. However, my parish only offered the sacrament during the afternoon on Saturdays. Since Tim and I had planned to attend a rodeo in Alma that evening, I would need to find other arrangements. So, after tending to my morning chores, I decided to drive into Gladwin.

When I arrived at Sacred Heart, the church was unlocked but empty. The priest had not arrived yet. Knowing that he could be called away for various reasons at any time, I decided to stay. I selected one of the wooden pews up front, knelt down on the padded kneeler, pulled out the rosary that was in my pocket, and began to pray.

For the past few weeks, I had been experiencing an unusual desire to pray more frequently throughout the day. I assumed it was because Judi, my mother-in-law, had been very ill.

THE ROSARY

The Rosary is an important prayer in the Catholic Church. Although it is considered a repetitive prayer by many, its purpose is to help a person meditate on the life and death of Jesus Christ. It consists of many vocal prayers such as the Apostle's Creed, Our Father, Hail Mary, and Salve Regina.

I was about halfway through my Rosary prayer when the priest arrived and graciously heard my confession. I always felt peace after receiving this sacrament, so I typically lingered in the quiet church for a few extra minutes before facing my hectic schedule. After going back to my seat, I finished praying the Rosary. Just as I was about to stand up to take my leave, a small prayer came to me. Whether this prayer was me asking God to encourage our second born, Nathan, to give up bull riding or God telling me Nate would be done bull riding, I was not sure. I continued to reflect on this as I made my leave. I had no idea that I would soon understand the saying, "Be careful what you wish for, lest it come true."

Returning from town, I began to work on the mountain of laundry piled next to the washing machine, a never-ending project for a family of seven. I made lunch in between loads. Since Nate had some free time after we ate, I asked, "Hey, Nate, why don't you grab your theology book so you can work on school?"

Unfortunately, Nate had not completed all of his work for the previous school year. Although he only had a few lessons to finish, it was not easy for him to find motivation during the summer months. "Ah . . . fine!" he reluctantly obliged. After grabbing his book, he joined me on the screened-in back porch so that we could enjoy the warm day.

As we started our discussion after sitting down in a couple chairs, it was not long before Nate's head started to bob forward and then jerk back. He apologized for his sudden case of narcolepsy, resituated himself in his seat, and attempted to listen again. Nate was like his dad in that whenever they sat still for too long, they would fall asleep. While I continued with the lesson, Nate dozed off again. This time I became frustrated. I debated whether or not I should actually get mad about the situation, when the words Let him sleep; he is going to need it descended onto my heart. So I surrendered my frustrations and quietly watched him rest. This time his head fell limply to his right shoulder.

Rearing Nathan was a little more challenging than raising his sister! He had colic at a very early age and was a handful for a few months. Unlike his sister, he did not have a good sleep schedule and tended to be a night owl. He soon grew out of that stage and was running around before we knew it. Boy did that kid like to run. It was at this time that I used to rub his feet and wonder what the good Lord had in store for him. With all his energy, I use to dream that maybe he would be a professional football player or an Olympic runner someday.

One summer just before Nathan turned two, we went camping at a state park up north with my parents. Because he would randomly disappear, we spent the whole weekend trying to keep track of Nathan. I laughed when my mom started saying, "Where's Waldo?" Waldo was a cartoon character in a series of search-and-find books that were quite popular with young kids at the time. The Where's Waldo series kept Dani occupied for hours whenever we travelled.

After about fifteen minutes, Nate lifted his head, realizing that he had been sleeping soundly this time. The seventeen-year-old sheepishly looked at me and said, "Sorry mom!" Glancing at the clock on his phone he added, "Oh! I gotta go."

I lowered my head and quietly replied, "I know."

I got up from my chair and walked back into the laundry room, which was by the back door. Nate stepped into the garage to gather his riding gear, leaving the back door open.

"Hey Mom," Nate hollered after a few minutes, "Have you seen my riding vest?"

"No, I have not. Where did you have it last?" I asked, while

I reached in the washing machine to move the wet clothes into the dryer.

"It must be at the bottom of my bag," Nate said.

"Nate," I stated firmly, "you cannot ride tonight if you cannot find it."

"Yeah, yeah! I know! Don't worry. I won't ride without a vest," Nate promised as he entered the laundry room and closed the door behind him.

Once he located his cowboy boots, Nate sat on a bench across from the washing machine. He still seemed tired as he slipped his feet into the boots. Afterward, he stood up. With his five-foot-ten stature, he stood almost as tall as his dad. He walked over, gave me a hug, and said, "I'll see ya soon. You're coming . . . right?"

His blue eyes twinkled in a teasing manner as I hesitated, looked up at him, shook my head, and said, "Nate, don't go! Don't ride today," I pleaded seriously. "You are too tired."

Not once had I ever said these words to him before. Even though I did not like him riding, I always felt that I had to bite my tongue. I was afraid that if I discouraged it, he would want to ride even more.

Nate put his cowboy hat on, hiding his thick, dark, wavy hair. He sighed and slowly responded to my plea. "I know. I kind of don't even want to ride tonight, but . . . " he paused, becoming more enthusiastic, "there are a lot of people coming to see me. I have to go!" With his charming grin, he gave me another quick hug and said, "I love ya."

Resigning myself to the fact that I could not change Nate's mind, I returned the hug and told him, "I love you, too." Then he hustled out the door toward the red minivan sitting in our driveway. Zack Donavan, a good friend, had volunteered to drive to the rodeo. Nate's brothers, Nick and Mathew, were tagging close behind. For the first time, they had convinced their big brother to let them go with him. I stood on the garage steps watching as the group piled into the van and drove away.

Tim and I had been living in western Michigan for almost eight years when I found out I was pregnant for our third child. With two kids and one on the way, we found ourselves longing to move closer to our own parents. We felt it was very important for our children to have a solid relationship with their grandparents. Then, as if by chance, a transfer position came available closer to Gladwin. Tim and I had twenty-four hours to decide if we wanted to make the move. So we packed up, sold our house, and moved back home.

Since I was six months pregnant and we were homeless, we moved in with my parents. My mom was more than thrilled to have a couple of her grandkids with her. I, of course, was very thankful to have help, though I was not sure who my mom spoiled more, the kids or me. As she tried to keep up with two very energetic young ones, she confessed, "Although I raised four of my own, I can see that I am out of practice."

About three months after our big move back to Mid Michigan, Nick was born, and Tim and I bought some property in rural Beaverton. It had a little two-bedroom trailer and a nice pole barn on it. Between Tim, some friends, and family, we managed to completely remodel the trailer by adding a shingled roof, a carport, and a large addition. In no time at all, the growing Davis family moved in.

It was about this time that Tim and I had to deal with an interesting problem. Nate, for the most part, was a quiet child. In fact, Dani did all of the talking for her little brother. Up until then, Tim and I had assumed that Nate could talk but just chose not to. We dealt with the situation patiently until his third birthday when we started to become more concerned. Tim decided something had to be done. One day, about a week before Nate's birthday, Tim looked Nate square in the eyes and, trying not to smile, said, "Nate, if you don't start talking, we will have to cancel your birthday!" Needless to say, Nathan thought his dad was quite serious and started talking immediately.

Nick, for the most part, was a happy baby. That changed as he entered the terrible twos. Although Nick was an incredible, sweet child, he was by far the most daring one I had ever seen. He was not afraid to jump down from or climb up anything. Because of this, it was challenging to keep him in a safe zone. Needless to say, I found myself exhausted by the end of each day.

Our little home's location provided us with the opportunity to attend three different school districts: Gladwin, Beaverton, and Clare. To both of our parents' surprise, Tim and I decided to homeschool. After much reflection, I decided that I wanted my children's education to be Christ-centered. I also wanted the freedom to attend daily Mass. So the Davis Academy was born with one star pupil: Danielle. Soon after, I found out that Mathew, our fourth child, would make his grand entrance into the world the following May.

Mathew proved to be a kind and patient child early on. Although he was quiet, like Nate, you could tell he was a deep thinker. Whenever I helped one of the older kids with school, Mathew would crawl up on my lap and assist me by holding the flash cards. I knew he was a little sponge, and this became apparent when it was time for him to learn to read. Reading came easy for him. He quickly mastered phonics because he had always helped me drill the other kids. He was not only bright but also courteous and trustworthy, even when his brothers took advantage of his goodness, as older siblings sometimes do.

Mathew was a few months old when Tim decided it was time to build a larger house. So before Mathew's first birthday, we moved into a new house that Tim designed and built himself. It was about a quarter mile behind our trailer on a different section of our property. It was a beautiful house, and the kids were so excited to have more room since we were quickly outgrowing our little trailer.

Once we moved, Tim's parents, Judi and Al, sold their house in town and moved into the trailer. It was nice to have them close by. Every day, once school started, the kids would walk to Grandma Davis's house after they finished their work to get an ice cream treat. That was one of Judi's biggest weaknesses; she could not say no to her grandkids.

Not long after my in-laws moved to the country, we started to farm. Our first farming venture was with a couple of pheasants and chickens. Grandma had other ideas, however. Judi wanted her grandkids to have horses, and she immediately went out and bought two. Hence, the Davis hobby farm was established when Tim and Al built a small barn to house our new additions.

In 2006, Andrew, the last of the Davis brood, was born. He truly was a bundle of joy. The kids were so excited to finally meet him that he always found himself in someone's arms. For the youngest, Andrew had the most determined personality. He, of course, had to keep up with everyone else. In spite of this, we soon recognized that he had a free spirit and danced to his own rhythm.

Nathan, nine years Andrew's senior, would often intervene as the peacemaker whenever Andrew's rhythm did not match my own. Because of this, Andrew adored Nate, and when Andrew was old enough to choose a sponsor for confirmation, he did not hesitate and promptly asked Nate to fill those shoes.

The kids grew bigger every year, and it seemed our farm did too. Soon, we had added a goat, guinea hens, rabbits, and cows to our barnyard. In the spring, the pigs had piglets and the chickens would hatch another batch of chicks. The kids enjoyed the animals so much that they participated in the Clare County 4-H every summer. Even though they did not achieve Grand Champion status, the kids learned many lifelong lessons like responsibility and hard work. It even proved to be a fruitful experience as Dani eventually decided pursue a medical career and the neighbors offered Nate a job milking cows at their small dairy farm when he turned fifteen.

Of course, farming was not the Davis family's sole focus. Church and school always came first! The kids were very involved in youth ministry, which included both church and community service projects. All of the boys also started with Cub Scouts and moved onto Boy Scouts, which I considered to be an extension of school. Later, Dani even participated in Venturing, a Boy Scouts of America program for older kids. These experiences provided further education, strong friendships, basic survival skills, an introduction to various job fields, and a strong sense for serving others.

Sports were another popular Davis family pastime. All the kids played T-ball. And as they grew older, they branched into other sporting areas. These activities seemed to be a problem for Nathan, however. He seemed to be prone to injury.

Although injuries are common in any sport, unusual accidents seemed to plague Nate. For instance, Nate took a serious pitch to the face his last year playing youth baseball, which instantly knocked him down but luckily not unconscious. As I watched the blood pour from his mouth, I jumped down from the bleachers to get to him. Despite the fact that his face swelled instantly, he was not seriously injured. After visiting the dentist, Nate learned that he would have to keep an eye on his front teeth from then on since damage to them could take years to surface.

Another incident happened while playing football. Again, getting tackled and sustaining injury is pretty common with this contact sport. This proved true for Nate when he took a slight hit to the knee during preseason practice for eighth-grade football. Coach Dan carefully assessed his knee and told him that he would not be allowed back on the football field until an MRI verified that his knee was not seriously damaged. With that news, we found a specialist who reluctantly agreed to order an MRI. The doctor was surprised after reviewing the results. He told us that Nate had sustained a very unusual break in the knee and if he had injured it further, he probably would have suffered permanent damage. The doctor complimented the coach for being so persistent. Had he not been, Nate's injury would have limited his ability to walk, or even bull ride for that matter.

So as our family grew and became more involved in the community, our lives became a bit crazy, but in a good way. The typical discipline problems aside, all of us tried to live our lives knowing, loving, and serving God. Through school, the kids learned about God and their faith. Dealing with the ups and downs of family life helped us learn to respect each other and to love deeply. Finally, by helping other people through church and scout activities, we learned to serve. Tim and I tried our best to raise God-fearing, close, and self-sufficient children while allowing them some freedom to pursue their own interests. As Tim has said so often, "We are truly blessed!"

Chapter 2

The New Sport

Be sincere of heart and steadfast,
and do not be impetuous in time of adversity[1]

A couple of hours after Nathan and the boys had left for the rodeo, Tim came home from work. He had just walked through our bedroom door when Nathan called to tell me that the rodeo was going to start at 6:00 p.m. rather than 7:00 p.m. I looked at the alarm clock that was sitting on our nightstand; it was almost 5:15 p.m.

"We can't make it, can we?" I asked Tim as I hung up the phone and set it down on the stand next to the clock. "We could miss Nate's ride even if we leave right now," I exclaimed, knowing that Alma was almost an hour south of Beaverton.

Nate sometimes rode as a fill-in, which meant that he would only ride if someone who had signed up did not show. Because of this, Tim and I debated whether we should go or not since there was no guarantee that he would even ride. After a few minutes of deliberation, we decided to go and

1. Sirach 2:2 (NABRE)

hope for the best. After all, it was a beautiful evening, and the drive would be enjoyable. So I finished getting ready as Tim changed out of his work clothes.

Knowing I was easily distracted, Tim encouraged me to hurry along. "Come on! Let's go if we are going to try to make it!"

I started to walk out of the house through the garage door just behind Tim when I suddenly realized that I had forgotten something. "I'll be right there," I told Tim.

"Hurry!" Tim replied.

"I will. I will!" I said, as I hurriedly turned back and ran into the house to retrieve a special necklace.

It was a Fatima medal on a long, silver chain that a friend had given me a year or so before. Laura Scheibert was the director of religious education for our church and had visited Fatima, Portugal, the summer prior. She had purchased a medal for each of the catechism teachers at Our Lady of Hope Catholic Church in Sanford, Michigan. It was very special to me because it not only had been a gift but also had a relic attached to the back of it.

I do not know why, but I had not worn the necklace before. I suppose I was afraid I would lose it; yet I felt compelled to wear it that evening. So I ran back through the house and up the stairs to our bedroom, opened the drawer to a small wooden jewelry box that sat on the nightstand next to the clock, and snatched the necklace. I then dashed back down the steps and out the back door. Tim and Andrew were patiently waiting for me in our Ford Expedition.

I quickly hopped into the front passenger seat as Andrew teased me and said, "It is about time!" The three of us laughed and away we went.

Homeschooling during the high school years was interesting. I found ninth grade especially difficult for the kids thanks to the heavy academic workload and crazy hormones raging within them. My ninth graders were the typical

RELICS

Relics are physical objects that have a direct association with the saints or with Our Lord. Scripture teaches us that God acts through relics, especially in terms of healing

- When the corpse of a man was touched to the bones of the prophet Elisha the man came back to life and rose to his feet (2 Kings 13:20-21).

- A woman was healed of her hemorrhage simply by touching the hem of Jesus's cloak (Matthew 9:20-22).

- The signs and wonders worked by the Apostles were so great that people would line the streets with the sick so that when Peter walked by at least his shadow might "touch" them (Acts 5:12-15).

- When handkerchiefs or aprons that had been touched to Paul were applied to the sick, the people were healed and evil spirits were driven out of them (Acts 19:11-12).

In each of these instances, God has brought about a healing using a material object. The vehicle for the healing was the touching of that object. It is very important to note, however, that the cause of the healing is God; the relics are a means through which He acts. In other words, relics are not magic. They do not contain a power that is their own, a power separate from God. Any good that comes about through a relic is God's doing. But the fact that God chooses to use the relics of saints to work healing and miracles tells us that He wants to draw our attention to the saints as "models and intercessors" (Catechism of the Catholic Church, 828). [2]

2. (Fr. Carlos Martins n.d.)

insecure students, not quite sure who they were or what they wanted out of life; thus they were easily frustrated. By tenth grade, the kids usually gained a small amount of confidence and found a rhythm to the high school expectations. That confidence usually lasted into the following year. At about the end of eleventh grade, panic would ensue, as there were too many decisions to make in such a short time. By their senior year, their confidence would set in as they formulated their plans for their future. During those last two years, they wanted and rightfully earned an abundant amount of freedom. It was a challenging yet fulfilling time as Tim and I watched them grow and adjust to some of their newfound freedoms.

By the time he was fifteen, Nate's social life primarily revolved around the 4-H crowd. Our neighbor Matt Badger, who was a year older than Nate, was part of that crowd. Matt and a few other friends had been involved in the Michigan High School Rodeo for a couple of years. They travelled all over Michigan to ride. A few of the kids even qualified for the National High School Finals Rodeo, which was produced by the National High School Rodeo Association and held in Wyoming at the time. These boys endured some minor injuries—broken bones and sprains—but nothing too serious.

The thrill of the sport soon lured Nate in too. Excited, he approached Tim and me one day and announced, "Mom, I want to ride!"

Surprised, I shook my head and said, "Absolutely not! It is too dangerous!"

As parents, Tim and I were not very excited by this news and discouraged it, especially in light of Nate's injury-prone sports history. Still, Nate would not take the word no for an answer. He was by no means rude or disrespectful about our discouragement, but he simply persisted, and halfway through the following summer, he convinced us to let him give it a try.

Nate started practicing to prepare for the final rodeo of the season in the fall. Because of this, I attended my first rodeo during the Clare County Fair that July. I went to see some of Nate's buddies ride. The rodeo clowns were entertaining, and I was impressed by the patriotic theme throughout the event. Yet, I found myself very uncomfortable sitting in the stands watching those kids climb onto such a crazy bull.

A few months later, I found myself anxiously watching another rodeo in Reed City where Nate would make his debut bull ride. It was a small affair, nothing like the one in Clare. After Nathan had signed up, Tim found out that Andrew was young enough to *mutton bust*. Mutton busting, as I soon learned, was when the little kids rode on the back of sheep. Andrew was leery about such an idea at first, but he decided to give it a try. I must say, it was hilarious. It was so comical watching the kids bounce up and down as the sheep trotted across the arena. Some even slid slowly down the animal's side, hanging on as long as possible before gently falling to the ground. Even though Andrew did not win, he enjoyed the experience.

Soon it would be my sixteen-year-old's turn to ride, but this time it would be on a bull and not a fuzzy lightweight sheep. I was extremely nervous as Tim and I took our places in the bleachers. I tried taking some pictures when Nate was waiting with Matt Badger off to the side of the arena, but I found myself needing to rest the camera on the arena fence because my hands were shaking so much. After a few competitors completed their rides, Nate started preparing for his own by putting on his gear, which consisted of a hockey-style helmet, cowboy boots with spurs, protective vest, leather chaps, and leather gloves. Even the sight of him with all that gear on did not calm my nerves. I suddenly felt my stomach knot up with tension as he lowered himself onto the bull.

Several riders surrounded him to make sure that everything was in order. After getting some last-minute instructions and securing his right hand on the rope, he nodded his head and raised his left hand to signal that he was ready. With music playing in the background, Nate and the bull were announced over the loud speaker. A cowboy from inside the arena pulled open the gate with a long rope and hastily jumped out of the way as the bull and its rider came out of the chute.

I held my breath. My heart pounded in my chest as I watched the bull lunge forward out of the gate. It kicked up its powerful hind legs jolting Nathan to one side. With that motion Nate slid off the bull's right side and fell to the ground. It was all over in about two seconds. Nate promptly jumped up and hopped the fence to safety, whereas the rodeo clowns stayed to distract the cantankerous bull.

After all of that craziness, I had hoped that this initial ride would prove to be too much excitement and that Nate would want to quit. That sure had been the case for me. But that would not be the case for Nate. His first ride coming to an abrupt end did not discourage him, and he eagerly continued to practice.

By the middle of the following summer, he had close to twenty rides under his belt. I always held my breath each time I watched. I would literally jump up, clap, and cheer after Nate fell off, bounced back up, and hopped the fence to safety. I remember just how hard one person who sat next to me at one of the local rodeos had laughed because of my actions. He assured me that everything would be fine. I knew I looked like an anxious, crazy mom, but I just could not find peace in such a sport. As fate would have it, my concerns would not go unwarranted.

CHAPTER 3

The Ride

Cling to him, do not leave him,
that you may prosper in your last days.[1]

The sun was still shining hot and bright in the large, outdoor arena when we finally arrived in Alma for the Gratiot County Fair just after 6:00 p.m. Once Tim paid the admission fee, we strolled into the arena to scan the crowd for one of the boys. As we searched for a familiar face, I noticed something strange. This arena did not have small rocks in it as other arenas had. "That is not too bad; that ground actually looks fluffy," I mentioned to Tim. "It would not be too unpleasant to fall on that." He rolled his eyes and chuckled at me while nodding his head in agreement.

After a minute or two, Mathew, Nick, and their friend Ray came up to greet us. "Hey Dad! You guys finally made it!" Nick said in a teasing tone.

Since they were on their way to the concession stand before the next round of events started, Mathew turned

1. Sirach 2:3 (NABRE)

23

and pointed toward the end of the bleachers directly to the left of the bull riding chutes and said, "We saved some seats over there."

Tim continued teasing the boys. "Stay away from those cowgirls," he said. "They are nothing but trouble."

"We will!" Mathew said jokingly and winked as Andrew, Tim, and I slowly made our way through the crowd to our appointed spot in the bleachers.

It was a full house and the seats were packed. Minutes after we sat down, Tim decided it was too crowded for him, so he stood up and made his way back down the bleachers to some metal gates that were part of the arena but to the left of the bleachers. I stayed seated to chat with a few of Nate's friends.

After the last round of the barrel racing event, I realized I would not be able to see Nate's ride from my position. Various pieces of equipment blocked parts of the arena from where I was sitting, limiting my view. I glanced over to see if there was room for me next to Tim. That was when I noticed that he was talking to someone. I did not recognize him at first. Oh! I thought to myself as a knot formed in my stomach. I realized that Tim was with Brad Doepker, who was dressed in his uniform.

Since this was a fairly new sport for us, we rarely knew anyone at the rodeos. I thought it odd to see Brad there. It was almost like an omen. How did he know Nate was going to ride this evening? Who told him? I suddenly felt waves of uneasiness and dread wash over me.

Brad, a longtime friend of the family, was the brother-in-law of Eric Johnston, one of Tim's high school buddies. The three guys always gathered together in the fall to duck hunt. Over the years, Brad became very close to our kids. Because of this long-standing friendship, we trusted Brad completely!

Brad was a seasoned paramedic. He was passionate about his job and very good at it. Many years ago, Brad's sister

Chris told me that Brad had struggled when he graduated high school. He was not sure what he wanted to do with his life. When she told me he was studying to be an EMT, and eventually a paramedic, she seemed very sure that this was what he was meant to do. Years later, his choice proved to have been a profound decision for Nathan.

Feeling nervous, I reluctantly joined the guys standing next to the arena. Andrew trailed behind me. "Hey Brad! What are you doing here?" I asked, trying not to sound apprehensive.

"Hi Michelle," Brad replied. "I am surprised to see you guys here. I decided to volunteer as the onsite paramedic today and—"

Tim interrupted Brad midsentence, pointing across the arena to the bull chutes where Nate sat on top of the metal fence near the bull he was about to ride. "He's up soon," Tim announced.

"I better get back to my station!" Brad stated as he started to walk behind the bull riding chutes toward the ambulance.

Nate had all his riding gear on except his vest. It was not in the bottom of his bag as he had assumed when he walked out of the house earlier that afternoon. Knowing that riding without a vest was not an option, Nate borrowed one from a fellow rider. This vest, however, was a little too short for his torso. Tim and I were unaware of this important fact as we stood in anticipation of Nate's ride.

Dissatisfied with my view, I moved to the left away from Tim and alongside the metal gates in search of a better position to see Nate's ride out of the chute. Peeking around a network of metal poles, I tried to get a better view. *DARN it all!* I just couldn't find a good spot. My efforts were too late. Nate was next.

A rodeo clown dressed in red tights with jean pants cut off just past the knees stood just inside the chute area of the arena anticipating the next ride. Nate quickly slid onto the bull's back and wrapped the rope tightly around his right hand. He instinctively raised his left hand above his head to help him keep his balance and to signal that he was ready. Seconds later, at precisely 7:09 p.m., the announcer called his name. The music started. Disaster struck.

A cowboy in the arena pulled the gate open. He swiftly moved out of the way as Nate and the caramel-colored bull named Vegas bounded out of the chute. The high-spirited Vegas sprang forward, crashing his head hard into the metal gate while kicking his hind legs up into the air in a fit of rage. Prepared for this jarring move, Nathan automatically adjusted his body and moved his lifted hand accordingly to maintain his balance while trying to find the bull's rhythm.

Unpredictably, Vegas lunged forward, clearing the gate while twisting his body to the right and pounding his front hooves onto the ground. He kicked his back legs more than six feet into the air this time and contorted his body to the left, throwing Nate off balance.

He is so high! I thought as life seemed to unexpectedly move in slow motion.

Nate struggled to regain his balance. He tried desperately to quickly shift his body weight back to the middle of the bull's back, but it was too late. Nate's weight suddenly became his enemy as he started to slide down the bull's left side. One more jolt was all it took to knock Nate completely off Vegas's back. Vegas took full advantage of the situation and, at the perfect moment, raised his head and delivered a dismounting blow.

As Vegas's hind legs shot up one more time, Nate fell. Still in midair, Vegas took his final revenge and drove his left hind hoof into Nathan's abdomen. In a fraction of a second, before I could fully comprehend what was happening, a cloud of brown dust swirled around them as the full weight of Vegas's hoof slammed Nate onto the ground.

I was stunned! "Did that really just happen?" I murmured

under my breath. I realized, almost immediately, that yes, Nate was just stomped on by a fifteen-hundred-pound bull.

Nate rolled from one side and then to the other grabbing his stomach!

Gripped with fear, I whispered to myself, "Come on Nate, get up!" I urged him again hoping my words could change the situation. "Come on Nate . . . get up before that beast comes back," I cried. "Don't be hurt! Please don't be hurt!"

With every second that went by, I tried to convince myself that everything would be okay. *Maybe I imagined it, I thought. Or . . . maybe it is not that bad. Maybe the bull nicked his side, and it looked worse than it actually is. I have seen riders take a hit. The clowns always help them up, and they always walk off. They have always been fine . . . nothing too serious.*

Little did Tim, I, or any of the spectators realize the damage Nathan sustained in that brief moment! To ease the crowd's tension, the announcer told some harmless joke at Nate's expense while two rodeo clowns came, scooped him up, and escorted him out of the arena. As the crowd roared with laughter, I kept thinking, *Stop! That is not funny! He is hurt! Everyone stop laughing!*

I looked back at Tim, who saw the sheer panic in my eyes. He calmly reassured me, "It will be all right. They got him up, and he walked off. Besides, Brad is there! He won't let anything happen to Nate. He will look Nate over to make sure he is okay!"

"All right!" I replied, as composed as I could be while trying not to panic. "You are probably right. After all, he did walk off, even if it was with help." Despite my self-reassurance, I found myself extremely anxious to see Nate with my own eyes. I wanted to make sure he was fine.

I turned and started walking with Tim and Andrew behind the bull chutes and past the holding pens. Mathew, Nick, and Ray ran ahead. I had never stepped foot behind the chutes before. I was seeing the large bulls up close as I walked swiftly around the corner of the fence.

Mathew nearly lost his breath as he bolted back to meet us. "Ma!" he said gasping. "It's bad. Come quickly!"

Horrified, I sprinted as fast as I could to the far side of the holding pens to be with Nate. My little heeled sandals kept slowing me down by sinking into the dirt. By the time I finally approached the scene, the rodeo clowns were practically carrying Nate toward the ambulance stretcher. Both of Nate's arms dangled around each clown's neck. His helmet had already been removed.

I was quiet for a moment as I paused to take in the scene. Strangely, I didn't see any blood. Brad calmly began to assess Nate. He asked him some questions so that he could understand the extent of Nate's injury.

When Tim arrived, Brad and Tim relieved the clowns so they could return to their duties. While the three of them stepped past me toward the stretcher, Nate intuitively reached out and grabbed my hand. Knowing I would be upset, he tried to reassure me. "I'm okay Mom. I'm okay."

Brad then started to ask Tim and me questions. "Are his immunizations up to date? Is he on any medications? Does he have any allergies?"

As they continued toward the ambulance, I turned to keep up with them and grabbed Nate's hand again, this time to comfort him. Dazed and confused, I harshly interrupted Brad. "Brad, is this a trip to the hospital?"

Brad nodded in affirmation, not trusting his voice. Because of his experience, he fully understood how critical his friend's condition had rapidly become. Nate's physical appearance changed right before our eyes. His face became white. He began to sweat profusely. Nate's body was reacting aggressively to the trauma he had just sustained. Brad finally steadied his voice and coolly stated, "Yeah, I think so!"

As Tim and Brad lowered Nate onto the stretcher, Nate blurted out, "Everything is black! I can't see . . . anything!"

My heart sank. *What does this mean?* I questioned, trying to stay calm. "Good decision," I muttered to Brad, staying as composed as I could. "So let's go! NOW," I insisted.

I walked quickly to the back of the ambulance. The back doors were already open, so I climbed in, expecting Nate to be right behind me. Sitting on the bench on the driver's side, I wondered what the holdup was and why Nate was not immediately placed next to me. I wondered, *Isn't that how it is done in the movies?* I had no idea that Tim, Brad, and the EMT were taking off the rest of Nate's riding gear. Antsy, I scanned the inside of the ambulance. It was emptier than I had expected. As I continued my inspection, I noticed a metal shelving unit behind the driver's seat filled with equipment foreign to me.

Needing a distraction, with my hands shaking, I pulled my cell phone from my side pocket and dialed my mom's phone number. It rang a few times before she answered.

"Mom," I blurted out, "Nate has been hurt. We do not know how badly yet! We are going to the hospital by ambulance. I will call you when I know more."

Her response did not even register in my head.

My parents were downstate in Cedar Springs visiting my youngest brother, Steve. Cedar Springs is located about twenty minutes north of Grand Rapids. Steve was in the process of remodeling a bathroom, and Dad had volunteered to give him a hand. They were planning on staying for a few days since it was a large project.

Steve and his wife, Lindsay, had two beautiful but very curious boys, four-year-old Gage and two-year-old Hudson. So while Steve and Dad worked, Mom helped Lindsay keep the boys occupied so they would not be underfoot.

After I called, Mom immediately went into the guest room, packed a couple of bags, and loaded them into the truck. Next, she interrupted the guys, who were very busy, and announced, "I am ready. Let's go."

Dad replied, "Just wait until Michelle calls back. We do not even know how serious the situation is or where Nate will be treated yet. No . . . we will wait until she calls us back again with more news."

As I hung up the phone, I became upset that Tim and Brad had not loaded Nate into the ambulance yet. Instinctively, to calm my fears, I began to pray. A few seconds later, I stood up and peeked out the ambulance's side door on the passenger's side facing Nate. "What is taking them so long?" I whispered to myself. "Pack him up, and let's go!" I muttered quietly, my impatience getting the best of me.

Unable to contain myself a minute more, I yelled out, "Okay," with urgency to the guys, "Load him up. Let's go NOW, please!"

Nobody heard me. I knew it. How could they? They were too busy. But I had to do something. I am the type of person that has to do something, especially during an emergency.

At this point, there was truly nothing for me to do but sit on the hard, metal bench and wait, so I said another prayer.

"Please Jesus, let Nate be all right. Please Mary, intercede for me!" I whispered. I looked to heaven and recited the Hail Mary prayer. *This must be pretty serious*, I thought as my stomach knotted up from anxiety.

After what seemed to be forever, Brad, Tim, and the EMT finally brought Nate to the back of the ambulance. They lifted him up and pushed him in beside me.

Brad climbed in and sat on the other bench as Tim hastily yelled to me, "I will meet you at the hospital with the boys."

I nodded to Tim in agreement and silently thanked God that Tim was there. There were many times he could not attend the rodeos due to his work schedule. I was especially grateful for his presence today since I was not in a condition to drive; besides, there was NO way anyone was going to peel me out of that ambulance.

HAIL MARY PRAYER

The Hail Mary prayer is composed of different verses taken from the Bible. Catholics use this prayer to ask Mary to intercede on their behalf before God.

Hail Mary, full of grace, the Lord is with you (Luke 1:28) . . . blessed art thou among women (Luke 1:41-42a) . . . blessed is the fruit of your womb, Jesus (Luke 1:42b) . . . Holy Mary, Mother of God (Luke 1:43) . . . Pray for us sinners, now and at the hour of death. Amen (John 2:5).[2]

The natural light outside disappeared as the metal doors slammed shut and the EMT slid into the driver's seat. I grabbed Nate's hand and started to talk to him. The ambulance promptly pulled onto the road. I heard the loud, sharp siren, which reminded me that this was not a terrible dream. This was really happening and my Nate was starting to lose consciousness.

"Stay with me Nate!" I urgently coaxed him as he slowly turned his head toward my voice. "Don't leave me!" I pleaded.

I looked at Brad. "How far?" I asked.

"Just a few minutes," he calmly answered.

I looked back at Nate's face while Brad's lifesaving instincts took over. He had already started Nate on two IV bags of fluid, one in each arm, dripping as fast as possible. When Brad checked Nate's blood pressure, it was only 80/50, even after two liters of fluid were pumped into his system. I, of course, did not understand any of this. I remained focused on Nate's face, oblivious to all of Brad's efforts.

All of a sudden, Nate began gasping for air. "Brad," I muttered in a panic, "he can't breathe! He is having trouble . . ."

2. (Eternal Word Television Network (EWTN) n.d.)

"It's okay," Brad reassured me. "It will be okay. That is why I am here."

He slid on the bench toward the front of the stretcher and reached across to my left side. He grabbed a mask from the shelving unit and placed it over Nate's face to help him breathe. Again, my focus was so centered on Nate that I was clueless to the fact that Brad was on the phone calling ahead to the hospital to advise them to activate the trauma team.

Because Gratiot Medical Center was a Level-III Trauma Center, it staffed an on-call trauma team. That means that they were not always at the hospital. When Brad called ahead, the team of surgeons, nurses, and technicians had five crucial minutes to prepare for our arrival. Little did we know that both the anesthesiologist and the trauma surgeon, Dr. Bonacci, just happened to be at the hospital already.

Oblivious to Brad, I became lost in my own thoughts and prayers. "Don't leave me Nate! Please, don't leave me!" I begged.

Minutes later, the ambulance pulled into the ER entrance of Gratiot Medical Center in Alma.

Nate made it alive!

Chapter 4

The ER

Accept whatever happens to you;
in periods of humiliation be patient.[1]

Nearly sixteen minutes after Nate was thrown from Vegas, Brad and the EMT swung the ambulance doors open and whisked my pale Nate away. I jumped out from the back of the ambulance as they wheeled the stretcher into the hospital. I walked numbly behind them feeling lost and in a fog. It was then that I noticed the strangest thing . . . my heels.

As I followed Brad into the ER, my heels annoyingly clicked on the hospital's bright-white tile floor. I rarely wore heels. Today, it turned out to be a foolish decision, since they were the only pair of shoes I had with me.

Doctors, nurses, and technicians had already gathered, anxiously awaiting Nathan's arrival. When I entered the crowded room, Tim came in behind me and instinctively put his right arm around my shoulder. We stood there in awe. It was 7:25 p.m.

1. Sirach 2:4 (NABRE)

A flurry of commotion surrounded Nate. I tried to peek around the medical staff to get a better look at what was going on when I noticed someone cutting Nate's blue jeans from the feet up.

DARN it all! There goes another pair of jeans. How many pairs have I had to buy this year? He is so hard on them, I thought. Feeling guilty, I began to self-reflect. Who thinks of such stupid things at a time like this? I wondered.

People started asking Tim and me all kinds of questions: "How did this happen?" "Is he allergic to anything?" "Are his immunizations up to date?" "Does he have any previous medical history?" "Who is his primary doctor?" "How much does he weigh?"

Although we answered the questions, my head was spinning. I was still trying to wrap my head around what I was seeing. With every second that passed, it seemed the situation became more and more serious. Tim and I were not even aware of the fact that Nate's blood pressure had dropped to a mere 37/14.

Without warning, Nate stopped breathing. The doctors swiftly moved into action as they tried to intubate him. Instinctively, Nate started to resist. He twisted and turned so much that it took five people to hold him down; two held his shoulders and two held his legs. Seeing that the ER team needed further assistance, Tim held Nate's feet firmly while calmly trying to coax him to relax. "Come on Nate, you have to let them do this! Relax, Bud!" After a few moments and another sedative, their efforts were successful. Nate was intubated!

Despite the fact that Nate had various tubes and IVs attached to him, the initial assessment did not reveal what or where the problem was. The anxiety of not knowing drove me crazy. Time seemed to be running out for Nate! I could not believe what was happening.

Understanding that Nate's current situation had become

desperate, I knew that I had to do something, something no mother would ever want to acknowledge. I pulled my cell phone from my pocket and called my mom again.

"Mom," I managed to say calmly. My hands began to shake once more. "Nate's hurt. It's bad. I need you to pull out the Three Very Beautiful Prayers and say them for me. I do not have the Pieta Prayer Book with me. They need to be said right now! Please mom."

THREE VERY BEAUTIFUL PRAYERS
The Three Very Beautiful Prayers that are listed in the Pieta Prayer Book are a group of prayers that are said for those in danger of dying. They are an appeal to the Mercy of God as they ask for forgiveness while offering words of comfort and peace to the dying person by reminding him or her how much Jesus loves them.

"Then Mom," I pleaded in desperation, as tears flooded my eyes, "call everyone . . . everyone you know, and ask them to pray. Have everyone you know call everyone they know and ask them to pray! It is the only way Mom . . . the only way he can make it! I gotta go now . . . I will call you when I can."

She replied, "I will. We are on our way."

I wiped the tears that were now freely streaming down my face. That was when Tim stepped out of the room to make his own phone call. He called his brother-in-law Bill. It was in that moment that Tim began to feel the full weight of his emotions wash over him. As he began to summarize what had happened for Bill, he felt his tears get the best of him, but only for a moment. After he hung up, he returned to Nate's room composed and ready to face what was to come.

When Tim returned, he stood next to Brad in the same spot he stood before. Brad had never left the room. Amid the commotion, the beeping noises, and the voices, he stood there and calmly explained to Tim what was happening. While Brad also assisted the ER team whenever he could, he was there supporting Tim emotionally even when he was not physically by his side. According to Tim, the experience was surreal. It was almost as if Brad was in two places at once.

With Tim there watching over everything again, I left. I had to find the boys. I needed to be with them. Somebody had to explain to them what was happening. They were waiting in the emergency lobby. I had to do something. I was going crazy, like a caged animal. I was so restless and helpless.

I found my way to the waiting room after Tim pointed me in the right direction. As I walked down the hall, I spotted large, wooden doors that led to the ER waiting room off to the right. I walked through the doors into a large, bright room. Our little group was there sitting on the edge of their seats, anxiously waiting for some news. Nick, Mathew, and Andrew stood up and rushed to my side. They silently put their arms around me and waited for an update. Zack—who had driven Nate to the rodeo—was there along with Nate's girlfriend Alicia and Alicia's cousin Ray. Each stood calmly by their seats.

"It does not look good!" I explained. "The doctors intubated him. They do not know what is wrong yet." My eyes began to tear up again. "Start praying everyone! Please!" I pleaded.

I gave the boys a quick hug, which gave me some strength, and then rushed back to the ER trauma room. Although the atmosphere continued to be noisy and hectic, I noticed that Tim still had not moved from Brad's side. While I stood there watching the commotion, I reached up and touched my necklace. *Was this why I was compelled to wear it?* I thought.

I took it off. Nate needed it. So the moment there was a break in the action and the doctors stepped out of the room, I took advantage of the situation and moved closer to the bed. I scanned Nathan to find an appropriate place to attach the medal. Jesus would, with Mary's intercession, protect him. I was sure of it. By attaching the medal to him, I surrendered Nathan's fate to Mary's intercessions. After all, Mary understood a mother's pain and would offer the most effective prayers to her son on my behalf.

"Maybe you could tape it onto his foot," Tim suggested after seeing what I was trying to do. Brad began searching for medical tape on some shelves behind them. He found some and handed a couple of pieces to Tim so that he could tape the medal onto Nathan's foot, which was literally the only place on Nate's body free from being poked or prodded. After he finished, Tim turned to the nurse and asked, "Could you please leave it there?"

With my task complete, and knowing that I needed to do my part spiritually, I marched back to the waiting room. I requested everyone to kneel so that they could pray the Rosary with me. The floor was hard and cool on my bare knees. I chose to wear a skirt that day because it had been such a warm afternoon. As soon as we started praying the Rosary, all sensation seemed to fade away and I no longer found the floor uncomfortable.

While everyone joined together to pray, my heart began to pray on its own. "Please God, be with Nate. Jesus, I trust in you! Holy Spirit, please heal him! Whatever it is . . ." I begged.

Interrupting us, Tim walked in and announced, "They are calling in a helicopter. They want to transport him to a different hospital. He needs a Level I trauma center."

"Where?" I asked getting up and rushing to his side.

"Probably . . . Grand Rapids," he replied.

This is not good, I thought.

The kids continued to pray. I immediately called my mom to tell her about the change in plans; the doctors had decided to airlift Nate to Butterworth Hospital in Grand Rapids. She announced that they would immediately turn around and head back to Grand Rapids.

At 8:15 p.m. the helicopter arrived. I followed Tim back to the ER when we were told the news, but I felt overwhelmed by the number of doctors and nurses in the room. It was so scary. There was so much commotion. I had no idea what everyone was doing. The walls seemed to be closing in on me.

To regain my composure, I stepped back out into the foyer, as if to remove myself from this awful reality. The ambulance distracted me. I was surprised to see it still parked at the emergency entrance. I also noticed that it was starting to get dark outside; that was exactly how I felt things were going for Nate, dark, yet getting darker (if that was even possible).

"Dani!" I said to myself, "I have not called Dani. She needs to know what is going on!"

I dreaded calling Dani. She and her friend Caley Meixner were on vacation visiting Dani's godmother, Michelle Gerow-Ellis, in Minnesota during spring break. Since Dani was a nursing student on a rigorous schedule, she had not had a break from school in almost a year. She was a hard worker and needed the mental break. I knew this information would devastate her, but I also knew that she needed to know what was happening, so I reluctantly pulled my phone out of my pocket to call her.

"Mom, what's going on? I tried to call you earlier but the phone just kept ringing!" Dani said frantically. She had briefly talked to Tim on the phone after he helped load Nate into the ambulance.

Guilt washed over me for not calling sooner. I thought to myself, *What mother forgets to call her only daughter in such an emergency?*

Desperately trying to control my emotions, I summed things up in broken sentences. "Nate's been in a bull riding accident. It's bad. Stay there. Grandpa Cassiday will arrange to fly you home. PLEASE DON'T DRIVE! I'll call you later. And Dani, PRAY! Tell everyone you know to pray!"

As fear continued to grip me, I reluctantly walked back to Nate's room. Tim gently reached for my hand and gave it a squeeze to try and comfort me. With my other hand, I reached out to touch Nate's foot to make sure the medal was still there.

"Mary will ask Jesus to take care of him." I reassured myself over and over.

Wrought with emotion, I let go of Tim's hand. This was too much to endure: to stand there and watch my lifeless son, my son who had always been so ambitious, hardworking, and constantly in motion. I turned to start down the hallway again back toward the waiting room to be with the rest of my boys. I had to do something to feel busy.

I barely made it halfway down the hall when Tim called out, "Michelle!"

I turned back, afraid of what he was going to say. Meeting me halfway, his voice shook while my heart sank as he relayed the latest news.

"He is not stable enough to fly. His vitals keep dropping. The doctors may have to open him up here. He is bleeding internally, and they cannot figure out why," he said grimly.

I looked up at him, stunned. His hazel eyes filled with just as much distress as that which filled my heart. Knowing this facility was not prepared for this type of situation, I questioned the medical team's decision. "Can this even be attempted here?"

Chapter 5

The Helicopter

For in fire gold is tested,
and the chosen, in the crucible of humiliation.[1]

After Tim finished sharing the news about Nate's emergency surgery, he hurried back to the ER. I continued on to the waiting room to update everyone. On my way, I called my mom. Yet again, I knew she was desperate to be with us, especially since the outcome did not look good.

"They can't fly!" I explained once she finally answered the phone.

"But we're almost to Grand Rapids!" she said, as if that would make a difference in the decision.

"The doctors have to open him up here! It's that bad Mom!" I stated.

"We are turning around right now!" she somberly replied. With that we both hung up.

After I joined the kids, I noticed the other patients and families in the waiting room for the first time. They were

---

1. Sirach 2:5 (NABRE)

sitting in a group of chairs to the left of the ones the boys had been occupying. Like a mother hen, I gathered everyone around to inform them that Nate was about to undergo emergency surgery. Not caring whether or not the other people in the waiting room would be bothered by our verbal actions, I encouraged everyone to kneel once again. This time we began to say the Chaplet of Divine Mercy.

THE CHAPLET OF DIVINE MERCY

The Chaplet of Divine Mercy is a devotion that is said with Rosary beads. It originated with Saint Mary Faustina Kowalska in the 1930s. While begging for God's mercy for a particular intention, Jesus spoke to her heart with these words:

"Eternal Father, I offer You the Body and Blood, Soul and Divinity of Your dearly beloved Son, Our Lord, Jesus Christ, in atonement for our sins and those of the whole world [repeated on the Our Father beads]; for the sake of His sorrowful Passion, have mercy on us...and on the whole world [repeated on the Hail Mary beads].

Jesus appeared to Saint Mary Faustina Kowalska many times throughout her life. During these visions, Jesus requested that she teach the world about his boundless love and mercy through this simple prayer. Catholics turn to this devotion in distressing situations, especially when facing death, for peace and comfort.[2]

As the words of the chaplet flowed out of my mouth, I could no longer hold back the flood of tears. The ache inside my heart could no longer be contained. It was too great! I was truly begging for mercy. "Please help Nate! Help the doctors!" I pleaded. As I recited the prayer, tears streamed

2. (Marians of the Immaculate Conception 2015)

uncontrollably down my face.

Tim rushed into the waiting room, interrupting our prayer. "The helicopter is ready. The doctors changed their minds. They think they should try . . . to fly," he stated and then left.

By then, everyone was overcome by emotion. As we finished praying, I quickly rose up to return to Nate's room. I had to see him before they loaded him onto the helicopter. I did not even make it to the door when Tim solemnly walked back in, this time with Brad. The dread on their faces said it all.

"They can't do it! They just cannot do it." Tim gravely announced as he shook his head. "He is just bleeding too much! They have to open him up here!"

At 8:28 p.m., Nate was transferred from the trauma room to emergency surgery. The medical team's choice to open him up on site was extremely risky for a few reasons. First, this was a new trauma facility that had not even completed its required certifications yet. Secondly, the medical team on staff had not dealt with such a case before. Thirdly, the closest blood bank was in Lansing, which was about fifty miles away. Surgery meant risking the chance that Nate could bleed to death because the hospital's blood supply was getting dangerously low. Finally, it was not a pediatric facility. Most rural ERs stabilize and transport serious patients, hoping for the best outcome. The doctors involved in Nate's case made a very gutsy decision to try to save his life. They had to choose to either operate under such conditions, which could at least buy some time if the surgery was successful, or risk the high probability of Nathan bleeding out during the flight. Neither choice was optimal.

I numbly followed Brad as he quietly led our group to another smaller room in a different part of the hospital. It was empty. I assumed that it must have been the surgery waiting room. In spite of not having any windows, it seemed cozier. It had carpet after all.

As we settled into our new surroundings, I glanced over at the kids. By then, Zack was a complete mess. He realized that this was Nate's last option. Andrew and Nick tried to be brave as they fought back their tears.

Mathew walked up to me and gave me a big bear hug, which I so desperately needed. Both of us had tears trickling down our cheeks. After he released me, I noticed a box of tissues on the table in between two chairs. I grabbed one, naively thinking it would magically hold back the emotions and the tears. Just then, a stranger stepped into the room.

Tim called me over to meet the stranger. He was tall, like Tim, and spoke in a calm, reassuring voice. Paul was the Spectrum Health Aero Med pilot, and as he introduced himself, he handed Tim a small red envelope containing some paperwork, which included directions to Butterworth Hospital, contact phone numbers, etc. Paul summarized the situation and explained what was about to happen.

"Nathan is in very, very critical condition," he explained.

"Nate's pulse and blood pressure are just too unstable to transfer him to a Level I trauma center in Grand Rapids, even after infusing many units of blood via a rapid infuser in the ER. It is imperative that the source of the bleeding be identified. Nate's surgeon, Dr. Bonacci, would have preferred to postpone this action until Nate arrives at Butterworth Hospital because of depleting blood bank resources here at Alma, but due to the seriousness of the situation, surgery was the only course of action," Paul explained. "After surgery we will immediately transport him to Grand Rapids. Once the helicopter lands at Butterworth, one of the flight nurses, Harry or Meghan, will call you to let you know that we have arrived, how Nate is doing, and what will happen next."

After a brief pause, Paul asked for our cell phone numbers. Tim and I gave him the information he needed and then he left.

By then I was beginning to get cold, very cold. My teeth

started to chatter a little. Someone had ordered pizza and breadsticks. I had not realized until then that the boys had not eaten since noon, and it was getting quite late. Thinking that the warm pizza would take the chill off, I grabbed a slice for myself.

"Who ordered this?" I numbly asked.

"Brad!" someone replied.

I thanked Brad but could not eat more than a bite. My stomach was in knots. A nauseating wave washed over me, so I placed the plate of pizza down on a small table next to the entrance. The boys were starving, however, and devoured the rest of the pizza. I was very grateful that Brad had thought about feeding them since food certainly had not crossed my mind.

"How long will this take?" I questioned anyone who would listen. If someone answered me, it did not register. I kept wondering and wandering aimlessly around the room. I fidgeted with the tissue that was still in my hand. As I paced the floor, I noticed that my shoes were not so loud; it was the carpet! I had not realized how annoyed I was from my stupid shoes. Why did I even care about such a thing?

Again, Tim remained calm. Again, he stood by Brad. Again, they discussed everything that was going on. Tim was handling the "rational" side of this situation. As for me, the mom, I was handling the "emotional" side with my heart, and it was breaking. To deal with my emotions, I kept wandering and pacing like a caged animal. I could not sit still.

By 9:25 p.m., a trauma nurse came out and told us it was time. "We are going to load Nate into the helicopter now," she explained. "Come and see him before he goes. Whatever you want to say, you will have to do it quickly while they are wheeling him down the hall. There is not much time! You must hurry!"

"Is he going to survive the trip? I asked.

No answer. No one would answer me! Yet, deep down, I

already knew their answer: no one expected him to make it. That was why the nurse insisted that each family member approach Nate to say our goodbyes. It would probably be our last.

"No," I told myself, clinging to my faith. "Mary will intercede for me and plead before the throne of God to spare him."

Tim and I stood in the hallway waiting anxiously while the boys remained in the waiting room.

"He's coming!" Tim stated. With trepidation he waved for the rest of the family to rush to the hallway.

Two flight nurses dressed in dark blue flight suits urgently wheeled Nate toward us. I approached Nate first and reached for his hand. It was cold.

This is just a dream, I told myself.

He was quite a sight. His thick, dark hair was a mess. Although he looked as though he was simply sleeping, he had several tubes connected to him that suggested otherwise.

"I love you Nate! You're in Mary's hands now. Like your guardian angel, she will protect you. I know it. I love you, and I will see you in Grand Rapids! Do you hear me? Grand Rapids!" I told him, hoping my words would help him fight against all odds for his life.

My heart ached. I looked up at Meghan and quietly pleaded in desperation with a quivering voice, "I want to ride with him! Please!"

"No," she tried to explain as sympathetically as she could, "there is not enough room on the helicopter. You cannot go with him. You will have to drive to Grand Rapids. It is not far from here. Someone will call you and let you know when he lands," she stated sternly, yet compassionately.

As Tim pulled me back out of the way so that the boys could talk to Nate, Meghan urgently said to me, "Oh . . . here! Take this!" She held out her closed fist.

Curiously, I stretched out my hand. It was the Fatima

medal that Tim had taped to Nate's foot.

"Oh, no!" I said, shaking my head and pushing her hand away, "You cannot give it to me. It has to stay with Nate."

She replied compassionately, "It will get lost on the flight. I cannot guarantee you will get it back."

"I don't care," I said defiantly. "It must stay on his foot. Mary will look after him! It must go with him!" I do not know where this small outpouring of confidence came from, but I was sure that Mary could influence her son Jesus, the Divine Physician, to save Nate. After all, Jesus turned water into wine at Mary's request. Why wouldn't he save Nate if Mary requested that too?

Tim, seeing my emotional reaction, emphasized to Meghan how important this was to me and asked that she just take the medal. He assured her that we were not concerned whether or not it got lost.

"Okay," she said reluctantly as she took it back.

We walked down the hall as far as we could with Nate. Each one of the boys—Nick, Mathew, and Andrew—told Nate how much he loved him.

Finally, Tim grabbed Nate's hand and said with a tight, hoarse voice, "Stay strong Nate! You got this! You hang in there! Love ya, Bud!"

We could not go any farther. After a moment, as we watched Harry and Meghan wheel Nate away from us, Tim used his shirt to dry the tears that had escaped his well-guarded emotions. It was truly agonizing!

When we could no longer see Nate, I seemed to lose my ability to think. Tim grabbed my hand and ushered all of us out of the waiting room. Our little crowd rushed back single file through the emergency lobby and out the entrance.

Once we were outside the hospital, I called my mom again and explained the situation with a heavy heart. "Mom, they are loading him . . . in the helicopter . . . right now," I sobbed.

"We are almost to Alma!" she said frantically. "Where

are they going to take him?"

"No . . . you have to turn around. They are taking him to Grand Rapids. You have to be there when he lands. Someone has to be there for him. He can't do this alone," I pleaded. Overcome with fear, I continued, "Tim and I won't get there fast enough. It's only a fifteen to twenty minute flight. That's it!" I sobbed. "They won't let me ride with him." I hesitated to try and control my voice. "You have to get there! Please!" I begged.

"We'll be there, Michelle!" she answered quietly, trying to control her own emotions. Then she hung up.

Tim led all of us to the parking lot. By then, it was very dark outside. I focused my attention on the ground to steady my footing as we cut through the landscaping to reach the Ford. Zack walked next to me. Everyone else silently followed behind. Suddenly, I noticed movement in the distance under the bright lights outside of the hospital entrance adjacent to the parking lot. As I looked up, my breath became trapped in my throat. Nathan was being wheeled out of the hospital. I glanced farther to the right and there it was! There the helicopter sat waiting to airlift Nate to Grand Rapids.

I dropped to my knees on a small patch of grass in between two parking lots. My hands fell on the cool, damp grass. I bowed my head knowing that I might never see my Nate again and that they were taking him away from me. *No! I do not want to be separated from him!* I thought.

I was overwhelmed with grief. Yet I knew, because Jesus taught us, that I had to submit, submit my will to his like I had never done before. "Thy will be done . . ." rang in my head over and over again like a church bell.

Tim, who turned around, gently bent down to help me to my feet. "Come. We have to leave," he said softly as he gently held me close to him. We were both in so much anguish. Yet somehow, Tim could function whereas I crumbled.

"No. I can't. I just can't. Not until they take him!" I sobbed.

My faith faltered again as I continued, "What if he doesn't make it. I have to stay until he is in the air! Please!" I begged.

It was so surreal to watch the team load Nate and climb into the helicopter. Although it sat there only briefly, it felt like forever. Determined to pull myself together for the long, excruciating ride, I dried my eyes with the wadded up tissue still in my hand.

I turned to Zack, who was standing beside me. I took a deep breath and calmly asked, "Can you drive? I mean, can you drive home . . . back to Gladwin? It is late. Will you be okay?"

"Yes," he answered, trying to be strong.

I gave him a big hug and took a step back and firmly looked him in the eye. "Tell everyone you know to pray! Everyone!" He nodded, not trusting his emotions enough to answer.

I started to move away and then hesitated. Turning back to Zack again, I briefly found my motherly voice. "And Zack . . . be careful! Take your time and drive safely," I said.

Without another word, I turned again to follow Tim. Once we were next to the Ford, we stood and watched as the helicopter's blades went thud, thud, thud against the dark night. After a few seconds the helicopter lifted and disappeared, taking my Nate and my broken heart with it.

CHAPTER 6

The Long Drive

Trust in God, and he will help you;
make your ways straight and hope in him.[1]

Ray left with Zack. Nick, Mathew, Andrew, and Alicia piled into our vehicle. Alicia had picked up Nate's belongings, which included his wallet, belt, phone, cowboy hat, and boots. I had not even considered these things. So with everyone and everything loaded, we started the agonizing drive to Grand Rapids.

Numbness spread over me once again, and I silently thanked God that Tim was able to drive. As he pulled onto the main road, I immediately began making phone calls. When it was safe, Tim started to call people as well. We asked everyone who answered to pray for Nate. Once we exhausted our contact lists, I asked everyone in the Ford to start praying another Rosary.

I was so distracted throughout our prayers. I couldn't help but notice how loud everyone kept sniffling as they tried

1. Sirach 2:6 (NABRE)

51

to hold back their tears. *Why is this taking so long? I thought. Why is this traffic so slow? Aren't we close to Grand Rapids? Didn't the nurse say it was only a fifteen- to twenty-minute drive? Why can't I pray right now?*

Praying was something the Davis family did often. Mathew was only four months old when disaster struck the United States on September 11, 2001. I remember the day well. The kids and I were sitting in a circle on the floor reading a story for school. Dani was seven, Nate was four and a half, and Nick was a bouncy two. We were right in the middle of story time when my mom called.

"Michelle," she said, "you have to turn on the TV." She knew that I was not a big fan of letting the kids sit in front of the television during the day. We had too many things to do: build with Legos, go for a nature walk, read a book, create a new craft, or learn how to cook. There was always a flurry of activities at our house, and Mom knew that I would have no idea what was going on in the world.

I jumped up from the floor of the small living room, which I also used as the kids' classroom, and turned on the TV. I was horrified! A few minutes later, a second plane crashed into the Twin Towers. I stood stunned and in disbelief as the smoke poured out of the buildings.

Dani was very perceptive and asked what was happening. I explained to her that two planes had just crashed into buildings in New York City. She asked if anyone was in the buildings, and I shook my head yes. Knowing that there was only one thing to do, the kids and I grouped together and started praying. We said the Chaplet of Divine Mercy for all the people that the tragedy affected and begged God for mercy on our country.

Over the years, many people would seek out my kids and ask them to pray for all kinds of special intentions. I pondered on that fact often. Jesus knew what he was talking about when he said, "Let the children come to me." It seemed that many of their prayers were answered.

Despite the fact that I knew this Rosary was more of a distraction for me, I had hoped that the kids were able to pray from their hearts. With all of the sniffling I heard, I doubted it.

I finally settled down. My mind quit wandering, and I slowly started to focus again. As I vocally repeated the prayers, my mind started to intimately converse with God once more.

"God," I pleaded, "he is a good kid! I know he is looking elsewhere right now as all kids do . . . but he has never been too far from you. I know he will do your work. Help him. Spare him. Be with him now. Guide those in charge of him. Hear my desperate plea . . ."

My phone rang, breaking my concentration. It was my mother. They had made it. They were at the hospital in Grand Rapids. They were waiting. "The chopper is almost here," she said.

I impatiently explained, "The flight nurse said that she would call me as soon as the helicopter landed, so I have to get off the phone."

As I hung up, the kids, Tim, and I continued praying. Everyone started sobbing a little louder as the tension thickened in the air once again. The unknown was killing all of us. I kept thinking, *Why hasn't the nurse called yet?*

All of a sudden, Tim, who had been pretty quiet, stated in an attempted humorous tone, "Slow down the crying please! I have to get us there safely, and it is hard to see when I too have so many tears in my eyes."

It worked! Everyone chuckled between sobs. That is one of Tim's best gifts. He can always find a way to make people smile.

The shrill ring of my phone interrupted the light moment. Almost instantly, tension filled the air. It was Mom. She had talked to one of the ER nurses. "Unfortunately, the doctors will not have time to call you," Mom explained. "Nate needs to get to the operating room immediately!"

Just as I hung up the phone with my mom, Meghan called. It was almost 10:00 p.m. "Stay on the line," she instructed. "He is just getting off the helicopter. They are bringing him in now. His vitals remained stable for the whole flight."

And then I heard a click and the phone went dead.

"Noooo!" I cried. "What is happening? How is his blood pressure? Is he going to pull through this? How can he?" My heart rapidly sank as I realized that the phone disconnected and my questions remained unanswered.

Again, I had to be patient. We were still a long way from Grand Rapids. Unfortunately, the faster Tim tried to drive, the slower we seemed to go. I was sure that only the slowest drivers were on the road that night, and we were stuck behind every one of them. I was confident that Tim would get us there safely since he had over twenty years of experience driving for the phone company. *Our guardian angels are keeping us safe,* I told myself, grasping for any distraction to calm my own nerves.

Mom called back almost immediately. "Nate was rushed to surgery," she promptly informed me. "He remained stable during the flight! Praise God!"

We would later find out that he was in the trauma bay for only five minutes. Remarkably, he was whisked to the operating room within sixteen minutes of his arrival.

"Find a priest, Mom!" I muttered. "Please! Just in case . . ." I finally verbalized what I had been dreading for some time. "He has to have last rites," I cried before I hung up.

As I placed my phone on the Ford's console, I found myself shivering uncontrollably without warning. Once more, I was very cold. It was then that I realized that I had not been breathing properly. I was only taking short, shallow breaths. I was hyperventilating. My legs and arms had a terrible, painful sensation. They were tingling; it was worse than that pins and needles sensation you get when one of your limbs falls asleep. I started to rub my legs and arms, but I could not stop the feeling. I leaned back in my seat and focused on breathing deeper, slowly in and slowly out. After a few minutes, the painful sensation started to subside.

LAST RITES

The *last rites* are the several sacraments that are given to someone in danger of death. These include Reconciliation (Confession), Anointing of the Sick, and Viaticum (Holy Communion). These and other ritual prayers and blessings, such as the Commendation of the Dying and the Apostolic Blessing for the Hour of Death, are part of the "last rites" by which the Church prepares the soul for death.[2]

At this point, Tim remembered that he had not called Jeff Bates, a longtime friend. Tim, after describing what had happened to Nate, assured Jeff that he did not need to drive to the hospital since it was so late. But before Tim hung up the phone, he made one request: "Please, please start praying."

Tim did not even have time to set his phone down when Jeff called back saying, "No . . . I am coming . . . I am on my way! I will not take no for an answer! What do you need?"

Tim asked Jeff if I could borrow a sweatshirt and sweat pants from Sheryl, his wife, because I was so cold and shivering. Jeff told Tim that he had already left but would swing by Meijer, a twenty-four-hour supermarket, to grab the items I needed.

We were not far from the hospital. Tim turned off the expressway onto College Avenue. As if he knew our location, Steve, my youngest brother, called to rattle off the last few directional details. When we approached the downtown area,

2. (Donovan 2001)

I noticed, for the first time, how tall the buildings were. *How many times have I been to Grand Rapids and never noticed this before?* I thought. Perhaps I noticed because it was so late at night and the buildings were all lit up. I found it peculiar how the mind works under such stress.

Finally, Tim made a left turn off Michigan Avenue onto Barclay Avenue. We were there! He pulled up in front of the Butterworth Hospital emergency entrance, which was part of Spectrum Health Medical Center. Tim instructed Nick to escort me to the ER doors.

I turned to tell Tim I would wait for him, but he simply stated, "Go! I have to park and the rest of the kids will come with me. Go!"

The long, awful drive was finally over! Yet, as Nick and I headed for the ER's glass doors, I wondered if any of us were really prepared for what lay ahead.

CHAPTER 7

The Wait

You that fear the Lord, wait for his mercy,
do not stray lest you fall.[1]

Nick and I rushed through the emergency entrance, where Steve had been waiting for us to guide us to the surgical waiting room since Butterworth Hospital was so enormous. Because he lived close to Grand Rapids, Steve made it to the hospital before the helicopter had even landed.

Seeing how anxious I was, Steve put his arm around me and said, "Let's wait until Tim gets here before we head up to the surgical floor."

I nodded my head in agreement even though every part of me wanted to scream, "Where's Nathan! I need to see my Nathan!" My emotions must have been written on my face because Steve calmly explained that all we could do at that point was wait patiently for news.

Frustrated, I gazed around the room. All at once, I noticed my aunt Marilyn waiting patiently. She ran over to embrace

---

1. Sirach 2:7 (NABRE)

me as soon as she saw me. She gave me one of those hugs that only moms would understand. I certainly had not expected her or my uncle Jim Cook and their youngest son Phil to be here.

"Thank you!" I said. "How is it that you are here?" I was surprised because my aunt and uncle also lived in Gladwin.

"We were visiting the boys," she replied. "I am so sorry Michelle! We are all praying for him!"

Aunt Marilyn had always been such a kind, sweet, and thoughtful person. When I was a child, she faithfully remembered to send birthday cards or pick up little knick-knacks for me. I admired her for her thoughtfulness. I found great comfort knowing she and Uncle Jim (my mom's brother) were there.

Tim finally came rushing through the doors with the kids trailing behind him. Now that we were all there, Steve led us to the elevators.

As the elevator swiftly moved up from one floor to another, I thought to myself, *What time is it . . . elevenish, maybe?* As we stepped out of the elevator onto the surgical floor, I noticed two big, silver swinging doors with windows almost shoulder height directly to the right of me. My mom and dad were standing there. I noticed how my mom held her rosary tightly in her hand as she prayed. Her face was filled with anxiety. As soon as they saw us, they rushed over and gave Tim and me reassuring hugs.

Steve pointed through the windows and said, "Nate is in there!" I walked over and peered in. I could see another hallway perpendicular to the door I was standing in front of. It had similar metal doors at the end of the hall. From time to time, I could see people moving on the other side of the window. I was hopeful to see something . . . anything to indicate that Nate was there, but alas, I could not. I stood there and silently prayed as tears fell down my cheeks once again. Dad put his arm around me.

"Help him Lord; give him strength and guide the doctors," my broken heart whispered.

Steve gently nudged us away as he said, "Come to the waiting room! You should not stand here and block the doorway."

I turned and followed Tim. Steve led us a few steps past the elevator and immediately turned right onto another hallway. The waiting room was directly to the left. The outside wall facing the hallway was lined with large floor-to-ceiling windows. It was a spacious room with a large TV in the middle of the far wall. To the right were chairs that lined the windowed walls. There were short walls in the middle of the room that divided it into three sections. This layout allowed for more seating. To the left of the doorway stood vending machines filled with snacks, pop, and water. Further into the room stood a help desk with a phone sitting on it. Past the help desk was a round table surrounded by chairs.

As we walked into the room, I felt completely overwhelmed. I assumed a few other family members would be there, but WOW! There were so many people. I never expected this, especially so late at night. Not only were my brother Jason, his wife, Kris, and their two kids waiting patiently for news but so were my cousins—Lori VanSlooten; her husband, Andy; Pat Cook; and Mike Cook and his wife, Jennie. Our close friends Jeff Bates from Big Rapids, Laura Llewellyn from Plainwell, and Marylou Sommerfeldt from Detroit were also there. As soon as Nathan's close friends Dean Schunk, Katie Hedrick, and Devon Poet heard about the accident, they made the long journey to be with us too!

After our friends and family greeted us, a representative from the hospital approached Tim and me. She explained how Nathan remained stable during flight and how the medical team rushed him into emergency surgery. She then asked if we had any questions or if there was anything she could do for us. I asked her if she could please try to contact a Catholic priest. I knew my mom had talked to Lori, who lived close to the hospital, about this, but so far no priest was available.

As Tim and I walked farther into the room, my mom walked over to an unfamiliar gentleman. He was a tall, middle-aged man dressed in casual business attire. He had a gentle look about him. Mom introduced him to me as Pastor John DeVries, a minister here at the hospital.

As Tim and I approached him, he said with sympathy, "The hospital asked me to come to be with you and your family." He paused struggling to find the right words. "I am very sorry to have to inform you that things do not look good for your son!" I caught my breath; it was another reality check even though we were aware of this. He continued, "I know you are Catholic and have requested a priest, but we have not been able to contact one. If you are willing, however, I can stay and pray with you."

My mom desperately looked at him and said, "Pastor, we greatly appreciate all prayers, especially right now!" He bent his head and led us in prayer.

When Pastor John finished, Tim and I thanked him for his kindness. Then I turned and asked everyone in the room to join me in praying the Rosary. Everyone accommodated my request and instinctively gathered in a circle, knelt down, and held hands. Since there were more than twenty-five people in the room, we took up most of the first section. I am sure we were quite a sight!

With Tim at my side, I started leading everyone in prayer by saying, "In the name of the Father, the Son, and the Holy Spirit, I believe in God . . ." While not everyone knew the prayer, they joined in to the best of their abilities. After calming myself, I once again slid into a deep, prayerful state and soon tuned out my surroundings.

Mary, please hear our prayers. Please, I beg of you. Intercede before the throne of God for us! I pleaded silently in my heart over and over again.

I did not realize it, but I was no longer leading the vocal prayers. My mother had taken over for me. We finally started the last prayer in the Rosary, the Memorare. My heart ached as the words flowed out of my mouth.

Remember, O most gracious Virgin Mary, that never was it known that anyone who fled to thy protection, implored thy help, or sought thy intercession was left unaided. Inspired with this confidence, I fly to thee, O Virgin of virgins, my Mother; to thee do I come; before thee I stand, sinful and sorrowful. O Mother of the Word Incarnate, despise not my petitions, but in thy mercy hear and answer me. Amen.

Once the Rosary was finished, I asked everyone to pray the Chaplet of Divine Mercy. This time I felt a need to alter the prayer.

Eternal Father, I offer you the body and blood, soul and divinity of your dearly beloved son, our Lord Jesus Christ, in atonement for my sins and those of the whole world; for the sake of his sorrowful passion, save Nathan.

Everyone quickly picked up the changes in the prayer and joined in. I could feel the communal plea for mercy as the prayer grew louder and more confident.

After we finished praying, small groups began to form. Soft conversations began while we waited. That was when Nate's friends Dean and Devon approached us. Distraught, Dean gave me a bear hug as he stated with an unsteady voice, "I want you to know . . . no matter what happens . . . I will always . . . always be there for the boys. I promise!"

Dean only lived a couple of miles from us, yet he and Nate did not become close friends until two years prior to the accident. Once they did, they were practically inseparable. On many nights, either Dean would show up at our house for a second dinner or Nate would go to Dean's house expecting the same treatment. Dean's mother, Jo, and I laughed whenever our paths crossed as we wondered how much food two teenage boys could consume. Because of that, we had already unofficially adopted Dean into our family. This moment permanently cemented his relationship with our family.

"Dean, you are such a good friend to all of us! Thank you," I cried and hugged him back.

Tim thanked Dean and Devon for coming, especially so late.

After that, I started to get antsy again. I needed to be doing something, so I walked out and made my way back to the big silver doors. I stood there peering in, wondering how much longer it would be until we heard some news. It was agonizing. My mom joined me; we both silently kept our prayerful vigil pacing and peering through the window.

Finally, after what seemed to be an eternity, my dad came looking for me; I could see the urgency in his expression.

"Michelle, the doctor is here. He is waiting to talk to you," he said.

He hastily led me down the dimmed hall and past the first turn to go into the waiting room. Click . . . click . . . click. Once again, my shoes echoed on the smooth floor. And again, I kept thinking just how loud they were. Again, I was evading reality.

Chapter 8

The Prognosis

You that fear the Lord, trust in him,
and your reward will not be lost.[1]

Dad led me to the next intersection past the waiting room. There was a lone fluorescent light trying its best but inadequately lighting the area where the men had gathered. Tim, Jeff, Steve, Jason, and Andy, who was also a doctor, were all there. Although light fell just behind the small group, there was just enough to spotlight a stranger dressed in baby blue.

Everyone appeared silent and somber. They were waiting for me to join them. I found the tension in the air suffocating. The stranger was not quite as tall as Tim. He leaned against a corner; the little hallway behind him was dark. His face reflected this darkness, as it appeared very grim. When my dad and I approached, I took my place next to Tim, who stood directly in front of the stranger. My dad stepped in behind me. The atmosphere filled with dread even before he spoke. His face was like stone as he glanced at the men gathered around

1. Sirach 2:8 (NABRE)

him. After a moment, his gaze finally came to rest on Tim. It was then that I realized that this man was avoiding direct eye contact with me. Knowing this, the knot in my stomach grew even tighter.

"I am Dr. Robertson," the stranger announced. He continued in a very professional voice, "We have done everything . . ." He paused.

Shaking his head he continued. "The liver just keeps bleeding. I can only get it to stop if I hold it together with my hands." He used hand gestures to show us what he meant. "Nathan has already had a lot of blood . . ."

This was too much for me. Feeling weak in the knees, I turned and moved to stand behind everyone . . . away from what I had feared. I felt sick to my stomach all of a sudden. I heard the doctor say more, but it seemed to be distant and foggy. I was not thinking clearly.

Dr. Robertson continued to explain that the surgeon at the Alma hospital could not locate the source of bleeding. Because of this, he stuffed Nate's abdomen with gauze packs to try to slow the bleeding.

"Once I started to slowly remove this packing, the blood began to pour out again," Dr. Robertson stated.

After further investigation, Dr. Robertson realized that the liver had almost been severed in two. Although stitches were possible for some liver injuries, he explained that they were not an option for Nathan because of the extent of the injury. Unfortunately, the only way the bleeding could be controlled was by direct hand pressure, which again was not a possibility.

"What about a transplant?" one of my brothers questioned.

Dr. Robertson explained that this would not be a transplant situation, since a person cannot live long without a liver. Even if he removed Nathan's liver to stop the bleeding, another liver wasn't available to replace it.

Astoundingly, Dr. Robertson had my full attention. I was drawn back into the conversation when I heard his next words.

"There may be . . . one more thing we can try. . . ." Dr. Robertson suggested hesitantly.

I never even heard the rest of his statement. I went numb again! My mind started screaming, *Why are you here. Why are you here? Why are you not trying this one more thing? You should not be here. Go!*

He continued addressing Tim, this time with a hint of hope in his eyes. Dr. Robertson explained a procedure that could block the blood supply to the severed part of the liver and, in turn, save Nathan's life.

"Will this work? Tim asked. "Have you ever seen a liver this damaged before?

With a bleak look on his face, Dr. Robertson replied that he had, twice; one patient survived and one did not!

I was not capable of hearing anymore. My brain reeled as Dr. Robertson's grim face haunted my thoughts. Those words pounded in my ears. *"We have done everything."* What did this mean? Was it true? Will I never see Nate again? Will I never experience his healing hugs when things are tough, when I am having a bad day? Will I ever be able to sigh with frustration as I peer into his perpetually messy room? How can this be? I need him!

I started walking back down the hallway, alone, toward the big operating room doors when I unexpectedly remembered how I had gone to church to receive the sacrament of reconciliation earlier that morning. During my prayer time, I asked God if perhaps he was telling me that it was time for Nate to stop bull riding. For fear of making the sport more enticing, I never asked Nate to stop. I had wanted to many times, but the decision had to come from Nate. It was then that I agreed and said, "Yes, it is time!" I had even suggested to God that I would be okay with a broken leg or arm, but not this!

"Not this," I cried abruptly as guilt washed over me. "I never agreed to this!"

Take me God, not Nate! I cried within myself. *He has too much work to do for you. He is such a kindhearted soul. He loves deeply. Not Nate! Take me! Take me instead!*

Distraught, I fell into the middle of the floor weeping and begging God again to spare Nate's life. *I will do whatever, God . . . whatever you want . . . if you save him!*

In a moment of weakness, I irrationally wondered if this awful situation was a payment for other desperate prayers made in my parenting career that had been answered. Yet, I knew that my God did not keep such scores!

But God, I continued my silent pleas to him, *remember Nate is Andrew's confirmation sponsor. Andrew still needs him! Is he even in your grace? He has not had last rites. You can't take him yet . . . please!*

I got up to move farther down the hallway. Where I was going, I did not know. I dropped to my knees again in pain and desperation. "Heavenly Father . . . if it be your will, spare my child. I know he is truly yours and always has been, but he is not eighteen yet. He is still in Tim's and my charge. We . . . I still need him!"

My dad came to me and tried to gently pick me up and offer comfort.

I pushed him away saying, "No! I am just praying! I am praying. Let me be!" It seemed as if I could find no comfort at that moment. My heart felt like it was being ripped out of my body.

Where is Tim? I suddenly thought to myself. *I need Tim!*

As if Dad knew what I was thinking, he gently explained to me that Tim went with the doctor to the radiology department. While helping me to my feet, he continued to explain that the doctor decided to try to stop the liver from bleeding by using titanium coils. These coils would cap the severed arteries in the liver and stop the bleeding. The doctor needed Tim to sign a release form. This procedure was truly the last attempt to save Nathan's life.

"I want to go!" I stammered like a little child.

"No, they would only allow one person to go. Tim will be in the room next to Nate," Dad explained in an attempt to reassure me.

Surprisingly, after a few moments and with a puzzled look on his face, as if an idea was being revealed, my dad slowly said, "He is . . . going to be . . . okay." And then with more confidence, he boldly stated, "He is going to be okay, Michelle! I do not know how I know this, but I am supposed to tell you. He is going to be all right!"

I was stunned! I was not sure how to take this. Was Dad just trying to be supportive? He had always been a realist, so for him to express this thought—especially when the doctor had clearly explained how bleak the situation was—was very out of character for him. I wanted to believe him, but I could not. I was afraid, afraid of false hope.

At that point, my mom approached us in the hallway. She hastily motioned for me to follow her. "Someone has found a priest," she explained. "He is here in the waiting room."

I wiped my eyes with my shirt and gathered myself enough to walk into the waiting room. There, standing by the vending machines, was an elderly man dressed in black with a white collar that matched his hair. Mom led me to him. I immediately thanked him for coming so late at night. As he shook my hand, he introduced himself as Father Donald E. Lomasiewicz from Saint Isidore Parish. It was just a few miles from the hospital.

Father Lomasiewicz asked, "Did you request last rites?"

I answered, "Yes, but Nathan was just taken to the interventional radiology department for a procedure. Can you still administer last rites?"

Seeing how distressed I was, he calmly reassured me, "It

is all right. I can still perform the ceremony with your family here in the waiting room. When the doctors allow it, I can anoint Nate."

He looked around and noticed a corner area with many chairs on the far side of the room. He motioned us to it as he said, "Let's sit over here."

As we made our way across the room, I realized that my other brother, Bryan, his wife Kelli, and their four kids had also arrived. They had been camping up north. They had been sightseeing on Mackinaw Island when they received the news late in the evening. They quickly rounded up the kids, who were scattered throughout the island. The last ferry of the day actually waited on them to shuttle them back to the mainland. Next, they packed up their camper in record time, about twenty minutes according to my twelve-year-old nephew Jake, and headed downstate for the five-hour drive to Grand Rapids.

Tim was the last to join the assembled crowd. Everyone was comfortably seated when I told Tim, "I miss Dani! I wish she was here."

With that, Tim dialed her number so that she could at least be part of the ceremony.

Dani and Caley had decided to drive back from Minnesota since they could not get a flight. Michelle Gerow-Ellis and her husband, Jeff, decided to follow the girls home. They were expected to arrive at the hospital around 6:00 a.m. I was very nervous for all of them to make the drive so late at night. I kept praying for God to send his angels to protect and watch over them too.

I had so many emotions running through me that I found it hard to concentrate as Father Don proceeded. I was exhausted! Slowly, I began to listen. A warm calm came over me. By the time he finished my anxiety had melted away. Peace! I had found a temporary repose knowing that Nate was in God's grace. Peace! What an amazing feeling.

In the midst of this calm atmosphere, not even ten minutes later, Dr. Robertson entered the waiting room. A few other doctors had joined him. Tim and I nervously approached the small team of men. Dr. Robertson stood quietly for a few seconds as the room grew silent. Then he looked at Tim and, with a glimmer of hope in his eyes, announced, "Nathan is stable." After a long pause, he continued, "I think he has a chance of making it through the night now!"

With tears of joy in my eyes, I whispered, "Thank you, God!" Tim wrapped his arms around me, and the whole room breathed a sigh of relief.

Giving us a few seconds to process this new information, Dr. Robertson continued telling us that Nate would be moved to the Surgical Intensive Care Unit (SICU) on the fourth floor of the Meijer Heart Center within the next half hour. After six grueling hours of anguish, Tim and I would finally be able to see our son. Praise God! Yet, moments later, this surge of excitement would soon be extinguished as we approached the SICU wing.

CHAPTER 9

The Directors of Surgery

You that fear the Lord, hope for good things,
for lasting joy and mercy.[1]

After the jubilant announcement, Father Don followed Dr. Robertson out of the surgical waiting room to complete the last rites ceremony by anointing Nathan.

Breathing a sigh of relief, everyone gathered their things. A nurse came to escort Tim and me via staff access to Nate's room. Everyone else had to use the main entrance, which required them to go down to the first floor, change elevators, and go back up to the fourth floor where the SICU was located. As we were leaving, Tim called Dani to let her know the good news.

Tim and I made our way to Nathan's room in the SICU moments after the staff wheeled him in. We anxiously walked in holding hands and our breath. We stopped. It was an overwhelming scene. He had tubes all over. The medical team had him hooked up to so many different machines.

1. Sirach 2:9 (NABRE)

Five different medication pumps hung on a metal rack that stood next to the bed by his head along with a ventilator, a VAC attached to his abdomen to drain the excess fluids, a monitor to track his vitals, and another monitor to check his bladder's internal pressure. These monitors hung above the head of the bed, but off to the right. It was quite a sight!

We slowly moved closer to the bed, becoming more aware of the noise. There was a constant beep . . . beep . . . beep in the room from the heart rate monitor. Every ten minutes the blood pressure cuff made a humming noise as it filled with air, indicating how stable Nate was. When it was empty, a medicine pump's alarm would sound signaling a need for more. To say he needed 24/7 care was an understatement. Later we would learn that Nate was literally the sickest person in the whole hospital for nearly two weeks!

I kept saying to myself, *My poor Nathan. This is awful! Please God, protect him. Jesus I trust in you! Mary, please intercede for us.*

The nurse looked too busy to even notice us as we approached the bed. After we stood there for a few seconds, taking it all in, the nurse offered us a seat. There were two chairs on the other side of Nate's bed: a comfortable reclining chair and a padded, wooden chair with a straight back. After checking on Nate, Tim quickly returned to the lobby to let everyone know Nate was settled.

By then many people in our support group had decided to make sleeping arrangements. Some went home. Others went to a hotel. Bryan and Kelli were able to secure a room at Helen DeVos Children's Hospital that was kept exclusively for the families of emergency patients. Marylou stayed with them. Steve, Jeff, Laura, Alicia, Brooke, and Nick stayed in the SICU family waiting room and slept on the couches.

After Tim left the room, I moved over to sit in the wooden chair. It was then that I noticed someone had taped the

Fatima medal onto Nate's bed. A slight smile of gratitude crossed my lips.

I watched as the nurse steadily worked. That was when a tall, middle-aged man wearing a white lab coat came in and introduced himself. "I am Dr. Carlos Rodriguez, Medical Director for Surgical Services here at Butterworth Hospital," he said. "You already met Dr. Robertson, the Medical Director for Surgical Services at Helen DeVos Children's Hospital. I assisted him during Nate's surgery tonight."

He had glasses and graying hair, but his most remarkable feature was his demeanor. Although he exuded an air of confidence, he seemed to be very gentle and kind while he shook my hand. As he stood there, watching the monitors, I could sense a genuineness about him. After this, he began to ask the nurse a few questions, questions I could not even begin to understand. When he finished, he turned his attention toward me and quietly motioned for me to follow him.

We stepped just outside Nate's room to the nurses' station, which consisted of a large countertop desk with a couple of tall, black swivel chairs next to it. This area had an enormous glass window looking into the SICU room that allowed a nurse to be able to observe the patient while taking notes. Next to the window sat a monitor displaying the same information that was on Nate's monitors. Dr. Rodriguez used his hands to motion for me to sit. I dully slid down into one of the more comfortable chairs. Dr. Rodriguez quietly sat down next to me and allowed me a moment to gather my thoughts.

After a brief moment, he candidly stated, "You know, your son is only alive right now because he is seventeen."

I quietly, yet, confidently refuted, "No Doctor! Nate is alive right now because so many people are praying for him!"

"Okay. Okay. Really," he said, sighing. He changed his tone to a more relaxed and faith-filled approach. "He is only alive because God does not want him right now. If it were you or me in there . . . well . . . we would not have made it. But he . . . he has youth on his side and that makes all the difference."

Dr. Rodriguez's expertise with trauma patients was broad. Many were fifteen- to twenty-five-year-old risk takers who believed that they were incapable of injury. He was amazed that Nate had survived the operation. From his perspective, Nate's liver damage was so severe that it was almost inconceivable to think a person could survive.

Tim returned just in time to hear Dr. Rodriguez summarize Nate's situation.

"The doctor who assessed Nate in Alma, Dr. Bonacci, was actually a former resident of mine and Dr. Robertson. I am very confident with Dr. Bonacci's abilities and decisions. Because Dr. Bonacci trained with us, the transition to Butterworth went much smoother than it would have had a doctor with a different background been caring for Nate."

Dr. Rodriguez, with a more serious tone, continued to tell us how Nate had been immediately taken from the trauma bay to the operating room in record time. Once again, Nate was given a massive blood transfusion. When he was stable enough, Dr. Robertson carefully removed the packs from Nate's pelvis and lower abdomen to assess the injury. Although this process caused even more bleeding, it soon became obvious that Nate had sustained a very extensive laceration on the liver's right lobe.

Dr. Rodriguez further explained, "To control the massive amount of bleeding, Dr. Robertson again placed multiple packs around the liver, putting pressure on all sides. At first, this seemed to slow the bleeding, so he used a VAC dressing to remove the fluid that kept pooling into his abdomen. Dr. Robertson was hopeful that this would be a sufficient solution until Nate became more stable. Unfortunately, the bleeding started again. At that point, the only other option was to try to send him to interventional radiology to embolize the hepatic artery."

I sat quietly trying to listen and comprehend all that Dr. Rodriguez was saying. Tim then told Dr. Rodriguez that he had to sign permission papers for that procedure. Nodding his head in agreement, Dr. Rodriguez continued, "Even though Nate was bleeding, Dr. Robertson was told that it would be almost a thirty-minute wait for interventional radiology. While waiting, the bleeding became worse and the VAC canister had to be changed three times. Nate became unstable once more, and his blood pressure dropped significantly in between more blood transfusions. That was when I came in to assist."

Dr. Rodriguez told us that there was still a fifteen-minute wait for interventional radiology. Since Nate was bleeding so much, they had to perform another exploration surgery. The only successful way to stop the bleeding was to hold the laceration together by hand. He said that they tried clamping the blood flow to the liver in what is known as the Pringle Maneuver and initially, it seemed to help, providing them with a better look at the injury.

"The downside to this," Dr. Rodriguez continued, "was that the clamping cuts off all the blood flowing to the liver, so we only had a thirty-minute window to evaluate the situation."

This was when they realized that the injury was too extensive and stitches were not an option. Next they tried to repack around the liver, but that was not as effective as direct hand pressure.

"Afterward," he continued, "we tried a Vicryl mesh sling, thinking that it would apply enough pressure, but Nathan was bleeding so profusely that the sling could not be properly placed around his liver. We removed the clamp for a few minutes and then placed it back on to try and buy more time."

Dr. Rodriguez then told us, "Packing the abdomen seemed to be the only solution, so instead of adding the

VAC, we simply closed the skin with whip stiches hoping Nate would develop some clotting again. Because there was still a significant amount of blood seeping through Nate's closed abdomen, we knew it was again pooling inside. It was truly a grave situation."

Not long after that, interventional radiology was finally ready. Even though Nate was very, very critical, the doctors transferred him from the OR to interventional radiology, agreeing to proceed anyway. It took two embolization attempts before the bleeding was finally controlled.

Taking a deep breath, Dr. Rodriguez finished with, "He is a very lucky young man. I will be around to check on him."

After thanking Dr. Rodriguez and shaking his hand, Tim and I meekly went back into the room and settled into the chairs. As we sat there, I could feel my chest pound when we heard the drumming of another Aero Med helicopter approaching the hospital. *That poor person. That poor family,* I thought to myself. Tim felt it too. He suggested that we offer a quick prayer for the victim. From that moment on, each time we heard the helicopter, no matter where we were or what we were doing, all of our family stopped for a moment and prayed for the injured person. Oh, how we could feel the victim's family's pain! We truly understood!

Time passed while Tim, in the recliner, and I, in the wooden chair, just sat, watched, listened, and quietly prayed through the flurry of motion that surrounded our son. Various thoughts troubled my mind. The most unsettling was the conversation I had had with Nate earlier in the day when I asked him not to ride. If I would have only known! I should have listened to my instincts! Forcing myself not to think about it, I looked over and noticed that Tim had dozed off. His head slowly fell forward. It was almost 6:00 a.m. on Sunday morning. Some movement in the doorway caught my eye. Dani had arrived! After driving through the night, she could finally see her best friend: her brother.

CHAPTER 10

The Complication

Consider the generations long past and see:
has anyone trusted in the Lord and been disappointed?¹

It had been the longest night of her life.

The girls, Dani and Caley, had been visiting Dani's godmother Michelle Gerow-Ellis in Minnesota for a little vacation. They had just sat down to order food in one of Michelle's favorite restaurants when Dani received a strange text message from her cousin that read: "Praying for your brother!"

"What?" Dani gasped out loud as she read the text. "What is going on?"

"What is the matter?" Michelle asked.

"I am not sure. I just got a strange text. It doesn't make sense," Dani replied.

She immediately called me. No answer. Then she received a pithy Snapchat message from Mathew. "Pray for Nate." Things were getting scary!

1. Sirach 2:10 (NABRE)

She immediately called Tim, who had just helped load Nate into the ambulance. "Dani, Nate has been hurt at the rodeo! We are in Alma. It looks like it could be pretty serious. I will call you when I can."

By then, the group's food had arrived. Dani was about ready to leave when Michelle's husband, Jeff, gently reminded her, "There is nothing you can do yet. You do not know what is going on. Let's wait until your dad calls before you make any decisions."

Everyone ate in silence except Dani, who sat staring at her phone wondering why no one was calling. Abruptly, Michelle's phone rang. It was my mom. Michelle stood up, and, as she went to pay the bill, she announced, "We are leaving. Now!"

Jeff drove everyone back to their house. Michelle called the airport to see if the girls could get a flight home. No luck. The girls packed up their things and left. Michelle and Jeff decided to follow them. It would be a long night!

It was almost 6:00 a.m. when she stepped out of the elevators and into the fourth-floor lobby. Gazing to her left, Dani was surprised to see Jeff Bates and her uncle Steve sleeping on chairs in the darkened SICU family waiting room. As she glanced about the room, she was amazed to see that so many people had stayed the night. She and Caley turned to their right and walked through the SICU doorway next to the information desk. The girls continued to walk down the long corridor to Nate's room. Surprise was replaced by dread as reality sank in.

Dani entered the room apprehensively. Tears filled her eyes. Moving from my chair, I rushed to her and wrapped my arms around her. We both stood there and quietly sobbed. Tim came over to comfort Dani with a hug as both of us dried our eyes and regained our composure.

Dani then glanced over her shoulder to find Caley still standing in the doorway. She was surprised since she expected Caley to head back to the waiting area with the others. While driving through the night, Caley had been having anxiety issues at the thought of entering a hospital. Caley's mom, Michele Meixner, had died a few years prior in a freak accident and Caley has suffered anxiety attacks ever since.

Caley's mom had been sitting in the metal bleachers at her son's track meet when he had stumbled on the track and taken a hard fall. Michele had jumped up to find out if he was all right when she lost her balance, fell, and hit her head. She was promptly taken to the hospital. She died despite lifesaving efforts, and Caley's last memory of her mom was in a hospital hooked up to all kinds of monitors.

The current situation was a scary sight to behold as the girls walked around the foot of the bed. Dani settled in the wooden chair that I had been sitting in next to Nate. Caley continued to stand next to the bed. Dani reached out for Nate's hand. He did not look like Nate. His face and neck were severely swollen from all of the fluids that the doctors had pumped into his system.

It was obvious from the determined look in Dani's eyes that she had taken up her post and was not planning on moving from her seat any time soon. Dani and the boys had always had a close relationship, and because of this, Dani was feeling very protective of her little brother. She did not want to leave his side. She knew Nate would feel the same if she was the one lying in that bed.

Michelle and Jeff walked in not long after Dani sat down. After all of us exchanged hugs, I gave a quick update. Michelle was shocked at the state she found Nate in, and she was amazed when I told her the details of how he had been able to pull through thus far. Tired, Jeff decided to rest in the waiting area after the long drive. Michelle chose to stay with me. She was a nurse, so she instinctively asked a few questions, but I was not able to answer them. I was relieved, however, when she was still present later that morning as a group of doctors and nurses gathered outside Nate's door. They were discussing Nate's condition. I stood in the doorway and tried to listen to the conversation.

After the meeting ended, the nurse came in and explained Nate's situation to Tim, Michelle, Dani, and me. "Although Nate is still very, very critical and receiving a lot of blood products, he remains stable."

We thanked her for the update and continued to sit quietly.

Sometime in the midmorning, exhausted, I finally meandered into the lobby. Tim and Dani stayed with Nate. Michelle, Jeff, Laura, Kris, Jay, Lindsay, Steve, Bryan, Kelli, and some of the kids were sitting around a couple of round tables talking while munching on yummy donuts Michelle and Jeff had thoughtfully brought for breakfast. As I made my way toward everyone, I noticed some long, brown leather couches off to the right. After giving everyone an update on Nate's condition, which had not changed, I sprawled out on one of the couches and fell fast asleep. At some point, a kind soul threw a blanket over me, which helped me to sleep very soundly for almost two and a half hours.

At 12:30 p.m., I woke up. I literally jumped up in a panic, gathered my senses, and rushed back to check on Nate. Again, not much had changed, except his blood pressure was slightly lower. The nurses did not seem to be too surprised by this. I reluctantly walked back to the lobby because Michelle had made me promise to return immediately so she could take me to the cafeteria. That was the last thing on my mind. Nevertheless, I relented simply because there had not been much change in Nate's condition.

From the waiting room, Michelle led me down the elevator to the first floor. We stepped out of the elevator into the Meijer Heart Center lobby. It was a spacious, bright lobby that consisted of white tiled floors. Tall windows covered nearly the entire wall facing the elevators. Looking through them, I noticed the busy traffic on Barclay Ave; it was the same road we had turned onto the night before to get to the ER's main entrance. As we crossed the floor, Michelle turned to the left and led me down a long hallway. I had no idea where I was going.

This is a huge hospital, I thought to myself.

Next we came to the main hospital entrance known as the Butterworth entrance. It had a large, glass revolving door with massive windows that surrounded it. This entrance led to the patient drop-off and valet areas. Even though the glass was tinted, I noticed how warm and sunny the day had become. This brief observation reminded me how so many things are taken for granted. It was a beautiful, typical day with busy people. I somberly thought to myself how everything can all change in an instant.

As Michelle continued to lead me, we turned left again. I saw some brown leather chairs off to the side just past a very long mahogany information desk. There were so many people coming and going. At once, feeling overwhelmed, I turned toward the chairs and dropped into the closest one. Michelle could see that I was experiencing a mini meltdown, so she patiently joined me.

"He is so sick," I said as I broke down into tears. "What if he does not make it? What will I do?" I asked.

"He is going to be all right. God's got this," Michelle replied tightly.

By the tone in her voice, I was not sure if she was convincing me or herself at that moment. Regardless, I greatly appreciated the hope and comfort she offered. I vowed to never underestimate the power of such kindness again. After we talked for a few minutes, I wiped my tears, stood up, and the two of us continued through the main lobby to the cafeteria.

Aimlessly, I followed Michelle once more. Inside the busy cafeteria, there were different stations set up along the walls.

One had a few hot meal choices. Another had muffins and bagels. On the other side stood a sandwich station. I slowly walked over to the sandwich area and chose a soft, flakey croissant. I then stood staring blankly at the rest of the food. Since I was not making any progress in choosing sandwich fixings, Michelle, like a mother guiding a child, asked me, "Do you want American cheese?"

I nodded.

"Okay," Michelle continued, "ham or turkey?"

"Ham," I said.

"Now choose some vegetables like lettuce, onion, or tomato," she said.

"Fine," I replied.

After Michelle selected something for herself, she paid for our food and found a quiet place for us to sit. The food looked tempting. Nonetheless, I could only eat about two bites before I felt sick again due to the wretched knot that seemed to have taken up a permanent residence in my stomach.

Michelle kept encouraging me. "Keep eating," she instructed. "If you do not eat, there will be two Davises up there in beds, and we can't have that!"

After lunch I was anxious to get back, so we returned to the SICU lobby where I joined Tim, who was standing in the corner talking to some people. A caseworker approached us. She invited us to sit so she could explain some of the insurance details, paperwork, and what to expect. She pretty much summed up what the doctors had already told us and asked if we had any questions. She informed us that because our family was Catholic, she could arrange for communion to be brought to us. I told her that would be wonderful. So, later that day, an extraordinary minister of the Eucharist met with our family, said a small prayer service, and distributed communion. For the duration of our time in both Butterworth and DeVos, almost daily, someone would seek us out to provide our family with the much-needed body of Christ. Again, I was grateful.

The rest of that afternoon consisted of visitors and plenty of praying. The lobby seemed to be in constant motion. Small groups of people would spend some time visiting with each other in Nathan's room. There was a constant stream of jokes and laughter, for this was how my family dealt with tense emotions, yet we were all acutely aware of how serious the situation was.

For goodness sake, he looked huge. Nate's neck was so swollen that he looked like an enormous linebacker on the Detroit Lions football team.

Because he was so swollen and in the Butterworth SICU, most of the staff did not realize that Nate was not an adult patient. Typically, patients under eighteen were placed in DeVos Children's Hospital Pediatric ICU, which was located in the building next door. But, this was not a typical situation. We would later learn that the medical teams made the decision to place Nate at Butterworth rather than DeVos for three reasons: First, Butterworth had 24/7 emergency staff that could handle Nate's particular condition. Second, it was closer to interventional radiology. Finally, it was closer to the blood bank. By then, Nate had received an astounding amount of blood products, approximately fifty-eight units in all (thirty-six packed red blood cells, sixteen fresh frozen plasma, and six five-pack platelets). For these reasons, the staff assumed Nate was older than he was, and they were quite surprised when we told them that he was only seventeen.

Since I had asked the nurses so many questions, I was beginning to have a better understanding of all the monitors and equipment connected to Nathan. I was so persistent with my questions that I was surprised when they did not banish me from the room for driving them crazy!

Most of the afternoon, Dani, Nick, Tim, and I sat by Nate's side. Now that I understood some of the monitors, I constantly watched the heart rate, blood pressure, oxygen level, and bladder pressure numbers. Even though Tim asked me to stop before I drove myself mad, I just could not. Nate's heart rate increased steadily despite the fact his blood pressure steadily fell. Of course, I did not know what levels were considered serious, but it seemed to me that things were not looking good, and no one said a word about it. As I became more and more anxious, I touched the Fatima medal that was still taped to the head of Nate's bed to calm my fears and asked Mary to continue to intercede on Nate's behalf.

By 6:00 p.m., people were preparing to go home. Bryan, Kelli, Jason, Kris, Lindsay, and Steve all had to work on Monday. The kids had hockey, soccer, and football practices. Mathew and Andrew were exhausted and decided to go with Kris. I, on the other hand, after watching the numbers on the monitor, became a train wreck again. I felt like something more sinister was looming in the air. Because of this, part of me did not want everyone to leave. As people gathered to say goodbye, I wanted to scream, "No, don't go!" yet I knew they had to.

Meanwhile, Dad took a very reluctant grandmother back to the hotel, and Dani and Nick decided to grab something to eat. After saying our goodbyes in the lobby, Tim and I went back to the room to be with Nate. I immediately pulled the wooden chair closer to the bed so I could sit and hold Nate's hand. Exhausted, I rested my head on the bed while I absorbed the sound of the steady beeping in the room.

As the monitors continued their resounding rhythms, my worst fears came to fruition. Nate's heart rate rose steadily and his blood pressure continued to drop dangerously low. Just then, my phone rang and startled me.

It was my mom. I moved from my bedside vigil to the hallway. It was as if I did not want my unconscious Nathan to hear what I was going to say.

"Mom," I said with a trembling voice, "I don't think

things are looking too good! You better come back. His blood pressure keeps dropping."

"We will be right there," she said.

In the time that I was talking with my mom, Tim had texted Dani to tell her and Nick to quickly come back. I then hung up the phone and anxiously stepped back into the room. In the few minutes I was in the hallway, things began to look very bleak, and the atmosphere in the room quickly changed. The more nurses that came into the room, the more fearful I became. There was so much commotion as they moved very quickly in and out of the room. I again reached out to touch the Fatima medal for hope and courage.

Mary provided the perfect example of hope and courage as she watched in agony as her own son, Jesus, suffered and died. With this in mind, I pulled out my rosary from my pocket and turned to Tim.

As the knot in my stomach grew tighter, I said, "It's time to pray the Rosary again!"

Tim joined me as I knelt next to the chairs at the foot of Nate's bed. We could feel the urgency in the room. After reciting a few prayers, Tim sensed that we were in the way so he shuffled me to the other side of Nate's bed up by his head, which was in a corner next to the privacy curtain.

"Please Mary, please beg God for his mercy. Ask him to send Saint Raphael, the angel of healing, to guide the situation and heal Nate!" I prayed in my heart as I repeated another Hail Mary prayer.

The activity surrounding Nate continued to increase as the kids entered the room. They immediately knelt down with Tim and me.

"Mom, what is going on?" Dani asked.

"He's crashing!" I intuitively replied.

We prayed while the nurses repositioned Nate's bed. His head was lower than the rest of his body in a Trendelenburg position. The nurses stood and watched to see if this would elevate Nate's blood pressure.

The four of us were huddled in a semicircle together praying when Mom and Dad walked into the room and joined us. Dad placed his hand on Tim's shoulder, a gesture of comfort and support.

I was no longer paying attention to what was happening in the room. I could not! I stopped looking at the monitors. I had no idea who or how many people were in the room. I blocked everything out, even the noise around me. I knew this was a desperate situation; I felt that, once again, the only hope was prayer. Nothing else existed at that moment, just me and my family pleading for my son's life. The only consolation I found that night was in the fact that Nate had already received last rites and was secured in God's grace.

"Will you spare him?" I asked the Divine Physician from my heart. "I know you can. I know all power belongs to you, but will you now?" I kept asking.

While I was unaware of what was happening, Tim was not. Though he did not quite understand each procedure's scope, he silently questioned what appeared to be an attempt to open Nathan's abdomen right there in the SICU room. He kept thinking, *This is not sterile! What is going on? How can they do this?*

That was when a nurse turned and urgently ordered us out of the room. Tim tugged at my shoulder and broke my meditation. I glanced up and noticed Dr. Rodriguez enter the room as Tim quietly and calmly told me that we had to move. They were going to draw the curtain, and we were in the way. They needed us to step out. But instead of stepping out with everyone else, I quickly backed up on my knees behind the curtain. I had to stay close to the thin fabric wall that separated me from my Nathan. I continued to pray. I kept hearing once again, *Thy will be done* in my head, over and over.

With all the activity in the room, none of us realized that Nate's blood pressure had dropped significantly. It hovered around 40/20. Because of this, the medical team gave him dobutamine, epinephrine, and vasopressin to try and stabilize his blood pressure. The situation was so critical that Nate received yet another blood transfusion.

"Mary," I pleaded, oblivious to the trauma team's lifesaving efforts, "be with Nate. I beg you." I was sure that Mary understood the tremendous pain I was feeling at that moment. After all, she stood at the foot of her son's cross. I hoped that she would continue to plead before her son with me.

How can he survive this? I asked myself, doubt taunting me while I recalled an earlier conversation with Dr. Robertson: " . . . right now surgery is not a good option."

No! I told myself, stifling the negative thoughts. *No more thinking. He is in God's hands now! We are doing all that we can do . . . But God* (my mind drifting back to prayer) *. . . I know he can do so many good things for you. He is a good kid! He has a heart of gold. As a boy, he was so close to you.* I pleaded as I had the night before.

I thought about a time when Nate was a little boy, maybe sevenish. I had taken all of the kids to Mass, and we stayed for a short time afterward for Eucharistic adoration. When I finished praying, I stepped out of the chapel with Mathew while the other attendees remained. After chatting with a friend, Nathan rushed out of the chapel to find me. Tears filled his eyes.

Deeply concerned, I bent down as he ran into my arms. "What is the matter?" I asked as I looked him over, thinking that he had fallen and hurt himself.

"All of a sudden I could feel Jesus," he said. "I had a warm fuzzy feeling all over, and it scared me. I think God wants me to be a priest!"

I simply smiled and gave him a reassuring hug. I was not sure how to respond to such a statement.

"See God, I know you have plans for him, maybe as a priest, maybe not. But I know he will do your work no matter what you have in store for him," I pleaded and continued to fight off the negative thoughts.

I vaguely realized at this point that Tim had gathered me up and ushered me out of the room into the hallway with everyone else. As I knelt with them in prayer, doubt continued its assault. Maybe he will not leave this room alive. *Maybe this is it. How can I say goodbye? Really? Goodbye?"*

No! I said to myself again, trying to shed the pessimism as I continued saying the Chaplet of Divine Mercy with everyone else. I had to hope in my faith. "You gave us this prayer, Jesus, to ask for mercy in situations such as this. It has been associated with at least two other miracles that I know of . . . but your will, God, not mine! I surrender Nathan to you!"

Although I had not even noticed, a nurse came over to talk with Tim before we could finish the prayer. Tim touched my shoulder to get my attention and motioned for us to leave the hallway area. My heart sank! What did this mean? Tim held my hand as I followed him listlessly down the hallway. He explained that the trauma team was going to wheel Nate upstairs for surgery.

I looked at him and whispered with dread, "Dr. Robertson said this would not be good."

"I know," Tim said as he gently cradled me in his arms.

"He said Nate needed to gain some strength before another surgery," I continued.

"I know!" Tim said patiently.

"How can he survive this?" I asked, knowing Tim did not have the answers.

How can I? I again thought to myself as my heart broke.

For the second night in a row, I felt as if I was living in the worst kind of nightmare and that there was no escape. Cold fear and doubt continued to surround me like a cloud of fog. Feeling emotionally drained, I numbly stated to Tim, "He's not going to make it out of the OR. I'm never going to see Nate again . . . am I?

Tim had no answers. His face was grave.

It was 9:30 p.m. Little did we know, another miracle had taken place right before us through the quick and bold hands of a second-year resident! But by the grace of God, Nate had cheated death for the second time in almost twenty-four hours.

Chapter 11

The Passage

Has anyone persevered in his fear and been forsaken?

Has anyone called upon him and been ignored?[1]

Tim led Dani, Nick, and me to some out-of-the-way elevators instead of the ones by the lobby. They were a little more secluded. Inundated with questions, I numbly followed his lead. *How could I be so calm at this moment? Shouldn't I be hysterical right now? Isn't that a mother's typical reaction under such circumstances?*

I tried to stop thinking such useless thoughts as I looked for my parents. Not seeing them, I assumed they must have taken a different route as we stood waiting for the elevator doors to open. As soon as we stepped into the elevator, Tim pressed the second floor button to take us back to the same dreadful room where we had spent most of the previous night. Knowing this, the dam of emotions broke all at once and tears streamed down my cheeks once again.

We stepped out of the elevators and walked toward the

1. Sirach 2:10 (NABRE)

familiar surgical waiting room. I wiped the tears away with my sleeve, and, as we walked through the doorway, I instantly found a small spark of hope. Our friends Michelle, Jeff, and Laura were already gathered in the waiting room kneeling, holding hands, and praying the Rosary!

I dropped to my knees with Tim, Dani, and Nick. As we prayed, more people filtered into the room: Mathew, Andrew, my parents, my brothers and their families, and serveral others. I was once again submerged in my own thoughts, wondering what was happening to my Nathan. It was then that I was moved to the deepest level of contemplative prayer that I had ever experienced before. My distraught heart felt as if it was truly at the foot of the cross. It was at that moment that I could visualize the scene. It was as if I was actually there. I stood to the right of the cross looking out as Jesus did upon the crowd. It was quiet. I could see the hard, white dusty ground and a few people in a distance watching, some in horror, others with curiosity. I could not see everything when I turned my head to my left, only the side of Jesus's feet up to his knees and the wooden cross that held them. His feet were close to me, at eye level actually. They were dirty and bloody. I reached out as if to touch them. I could not. They were just out of reach. Yet I could feel the pain.

I whispered, "Mary, I am at the foot of the cross with you. This is too hard to endure."

A hand reach out and settle on my left shoulder. I did not see her, but I felt like Mary was supporting me. The words *I am here* and *yes you can* settle over me. *Is this my imagination?* I wondered.

And with that, the image was gone. I was back in the present, aware of what was going on in the waiting room as our group of prayer warriors continued their pleas. Again as I heard everyone's words end the Divine Mercy Chaplet, I repeated, "Mary, I am still at the foot of Jesus's cross with you; help me . . . pray for me so that I may endure God's will."

Once the group finished the last prayer, everyone slowly stood up. I turned to Tim, who put his arms around me. As I leaned into him, I started to softly sing:

Teach my song to rise to you
When temptation comes my way
And when I cannot stand I'll fall on you
Jesus, you're my hope and stay

I probably sounded ridiculous reciting the lyrics to Matt Maher's song "Lord I Need You." I was, afterall, sobbing through the whole song, but I did not care. It was so reassuring to have Tim hold me with Matt Maher's song occupying my thoughts. How many times had I played that CD in the Ford over the past year? Although the boys had grown weary of hearing it, I continued to play it. The song reminded me that God was bigger than the problems of life. I had no idea how hard I would lean on that song, those words, and Tim's support to help me through such excruciating moments.

When I finished, Tim hugged me once again. Upon his release, I felt this indescribable, warm peace settle over me. I wiped my tears and took a big, long breath and thought, *Okay, it's all okay. No matter what happens, it will be okay.*

While a few people came up to console Tim and me, I scanned the room and realized that everyone who had left had returned. We had so much unconditional support and were truly blessed! I could not imagine facing this alone. As I walked around thanking everyone, I noticed even more of Nate's friends had joined us. *When did they arrive?* I wondered to myself, touched by their mere presence. I never dreamed this many of Nate's friends would be here given the distance. And there they were, joining our already large support group as we stormed the gates of heaven. I knew I would forever be indebted to everyone who was present. I was later told that more than forty people had gathered in the waiting room that Sunday night.

Feeling calmer, I decided to seek out some isolation if only for a few moments. I returned to what I considered my personal waiting post, the corner next to the big silver doors that opened to the surgery wing across from the elevators. Before leaning against the corner wall and slowly sliding to the floor in a sitting position, I walked to the doors and peeked through the windows, hopeful to see something. Alas, there was nothing to see.

I sat alone patiently staring at the elevator doors waiting for some news when I began to focus on something positive: *No news is good news! He has been in the OR for quite some time. This must be a good thing, right?*

Because I was deep in thought, Jeff Bates startled me when he approached and said, "Oh, there you are! Mind if I join you?"

"Of course," I replied and scooted over so he could sit against the wall.

"Here," he said as he handed me his phone. "As you know, Sheryl is at home with the kids, but she wanted to share something with you."

"Okay," I agreed.

Expecting a short note of encouragement, I was surprised to see a lengthy passage and wondered to myself if I could stay focused as I started to read. At first, I did not recognize the passage. I began to find some comfort in it.

1. For the leader. A song of the Korahites. According to alamoth.

2. God is our refuge and our strength, an ever-present help in distress.

3. Thus we do not fear, though earth be shaken and mountains quake to the depths of the sea,

4. Though its waters rage and foam and mountains totter at its surging. *Selah*

5. Streams of the river gladden the city of God, the holy dwelling of the Most High.

6. God is in its midst; it shall not be shaken; God will help it at break of day.

7. Though nations rage and kingdoms totter, he utters his voice and the earth melts.

8. The LORD of hosts is with us; our stronghold is the God of Jacob. *Selah*

9. Come and see the works of the LORD, who has done fearsome deeds on earth;

10. Who stops wars to the ends of the earth, breaks the bow, splinters the spear, and burns the shields with fire;[2]

It was not until I read the eleventh verse that I recognized the hand of God. Yes, I knew that we were surrounded by the love of family and friends, and I greatly appreciated that. I knew that this love was a direct affirmation of God's presence, but reading this verse had a profound effect on me. This verse confirmed, in a very private way, that he had not forsaken me, Nate, or my family.

11 "Be still and know that I am God! I am exalted among the nations, exalted on the earth."

12 The LORD of hosts is with us; our stronghold is the God of Jacob. *Selah*[3]

I was stunned, for verse eleven was my favorite bible verse. I did not even realized it was part of Psalm 46. I had prayerfully repeated it on many occasions as it helped me push through many challenging moments thus far during

2. (United States Conference of Catholic Bishops n.d.)
3. (United States Conference of Catholic Bishops n.d.)

my parenting career. I had used it often to remind myself that God was in control and he would guide me if I let him. It was such a short and sweet verse that I had added it to the bottom section of every page in the daily school lesson planner that I created at the beginning of each school year. Many times I would read "Be still and know that I am God" silently as I listed each child's work for the day. It brought me peace among the chaos that came with homeschooling five children.

Since this was not common knowledge, I wondered *How did Sheryl know? How could she have known?* Here, without even seeking such counsel, God provided me with his word in such a way that was clearly telling me that he was in control and I should sit back and let him take care of everything. I was not in control, so I just had to surrender everything to him.

I hugged Jeff and said, "Thank you; you have no idea what you have just done for me." While standing up, I proceeded to tell him the significance of what he shared.

As Jeff and I were finishing our discussion, Tim, Steve, and Mom joined us.

"There you are," Mom said to me. "I was wondering where you disappeared to."

"Sorry, I just needed a few moments away from everyone," I replied.

Just then, the elevator dinged. The four of us looked up as the doors opened. Out walked Aunt Shirley and Aunt Jean, my father's sisters. I was relieved to see them. It was almost as if I had expected them to come. I was not sure why, since it was such a long drive from Gladwin and it was so late at night.

As soon as they stepped out of the elevator, they both embraced Tim and me.

"I am glad you're here," I told them.

Aunt Jean looked at me and said, "It was the strangest thing. Shirley called me just as I was driving home from

Lansing and told me that Nate had taken a turn for the worse. She informed me that she was going to stop by and pick me up on her way down to the hospital. Even though your dad told her not to come, she felt it was imperative that we hurry."

"Thanks for coming," was Tim's response.

Aunt Shirley, a very spiritual person, said, "Hold hands please. I feel a strong need to pray now!"

Her words were short but powerful. She glorified God and urged God to guide the surgeons' hands while bestowing wisdom on them and all of the hospital staff who were caring for Nate. She finished the prayer pleading our Father God to completely heal Nathan if it was according to his divine will. Everyone was deeply moved by her words. When she finished, she shook from the intensity and urgency of her prayer. Seeing this, Steve gently reached out to steady her.

Once Aunt Shirley relaxed, Mom updated both of them on what we knew, which was not much. It was then that I realized that Tim had disappeared. During Mom's briefing, in silence, he walked away. A slight movement caught the corner of my eye. I glanced down the hallway where Dr. Robertson had given us the bleak news the night before. There he was, alone and pacing. I could see that he was struggling to maintain his composure.

I thought to myself, *He needs me. Tim actually needs me.* I quickly hurried over to him. He had been so strong up until this point that it was hard to imagine a crack in the rock.

As I approached, he turned away from me and stretched out his hand as if to hold me back. He shook his head and choked out the words "Not now!"

Tears again welled up in my eyes. I could see that Tim was on the verge of a breakdown. I grabbed his hand, pulled him around to me, and embraced him. In that instant, I realized that I had been so selfishly caught up in my own grief that I had not reached out to comfort my own husband. Up until then, he had been comforting me, reaching out to me when I needed it. I had not returned the gesture. It was my turn to be there for him, to help him deal with the anguish. Slowly, the tension melted as we just stood there all alone, holding each other, drawing strength from each other. In that brief moment, I realized how tragedies could severely hinder a couple's relationship if they did not find a way to grieve together.

Slowly, feeling more poised, we turned around and walked back to the waiting room together. By now, people were standing around talking, waiting patiently for any word. No news was good news, or so I hoped.

I had not noticed until then that my second cousin Ryan, Aunt Shirley's grandson, had also joined us. He was staying in Grand Rapids because he had been playing baseball for the triple A Detroit Tigers team known as the West Michigan Whitecaps. A group had gathered around him as he updated everyone on his pitching adventures. It was nice to hear how well he was doing. During the discussions, he invited all of the younger cousins to come to see him pitch. He was scheduled to pitch during the next few games. Of course, smiles brightened the kids' faces as they thought that this was an outstanding idea. Ryan was so considerate to offer such a delightful diversion. It reminded me of how God can sprinkle goodness throughout the pain.

With so many friends and family members gathered, and because we still had no word about Nate, Dad suggested that we needed another group prayer. "Shirley, will you lead us?" he asked.

"Absolutely," she replied.

Everyone gathered together holding hands and formed a huge circle, which took up a good portion of the waiting room and entrance. Shirley started by praising God for all of the strength and support from those who had gathered for a second time at the hospital so late at night for Nathan. Her prayer was confident and firm as she stated that she knew

God's almighty power could touch Nathan and heal him. She continued by stating that she knew the Holy Spirit would guide the surgeons and their staff to find any unresolved issues concerning Nathan. She asked Father God to bestow wisdom upon the doctors to repair Nate's liver and restore his health. She continued to praise God with an undeniable love for him. Finally, she thanked Father God, knowing that he would hear and answer these prayers.

This prayer was quite different from the earlier Rosary and Chaplet prayers, which were prayers of pleading and acceptance of God's will. This latest prayer united everyone present in what can only be described as pure confidence. Through this confidence, the room was once again transformed with a powerful sense of supernatural hope. Everyone present was deeply affected by Aunt Shirley's words. Serenity washed over us. It was incredible how this tranquility seemed to settle over everyone—not just some, but everyone. It had to be the effects of prayer, a gift given through the Holy Spirit!

As the crowd once again dispersed into smaller groups, I hugged Aunt Shirley and said, "Thanks. You know we have to stop meeting under these circumstances!" Aunt Shirley's own teenage granddaughter had recently been released from the ICU at University of Michigan Hospital in Ann Arbor. That too had been quite a bleak situation, but, by the grace of God, her granddaughter had recovered and was doing amazingly well at home. This fact also brought me great hope.

During this conversation, I recalled how I had spoken to my cousin and his wife while visiting their daughter in the ICU. We had talked about different circumstances surrounding her condition. I told my cousin, "If any of my kids were in such a desperate situation, I would call everyone and ask them to pray. Why, I would ask them to call all of their friends and ask them to pray too." Those words turned out to be quite prophetic just a few weeks later.

Our conversation was interrupted by my cell phone's sharp ring. I excused myself and moved to the hallway to answer it when I received a pleasant surprise. It was Darla Nickels.

Tim and I used to live near Darla many years ago when we lived in southwest Michigan. After we moved to Clare County, Darla and I had rarely seen each other, but we tried to keep in touch as often as we could. She informed me that her son Stephen, who was a Facebook friend with Dani, told her about Nathan's critical condition. I shared with her all of the details surrounding the accident, how he barely made it through Saturday night, and how he was actually in emergency surgery as we spoke.

She said, "I have been praying for Nate since I heard the news. I can't come to visit until Tuesday morning, but I wanted you to know that Nate is going to be fine. He is going to make it. I am sure of it."

I asked, "How can you possibly know such a thing?"

She hesitated and then said, "I have something you need to see. I will bring it when I come. You will understand then." She reassured me again before saying goodbye. "Nate is going to be fine. Everything will be all right. I will see you soon."

By then, it was well after midnight, and people continued to visit quietly. The mood in the room remained calm and quite peaceful when, at last, the highly anticipated moment arrived.

Dr. Robertson, who was again dressed in light blue and was wearing his surgical hat and mask, walked in. Tim and I approached him. The atmosphere in the room turned tense. Dr. Robertson's mask was pulled down around his neck and off to the side. Tonight his mood seemed different. He looked right at me! I held my breath in anticipation. Instead of the dark, intense look he had the night before, he had a hint of confidence about him; a glimmer of hope emanated from his eyes.

He looked directly at Tim and asked if he wanted to find a quiet room where the three of us could talk privately. Tim quickly scanned the room, which was filled with anxious people. "No, you can tell us what needs to be said right here."

With those words, the room filled with a deafening silence. Dr. Robertson glanced down momentarily, as if he was trying to find the proper words to say. After gathering his thoughts, his attention returned to his audience. "I think he's going to make it!" he announced. A small smile crept through his professional guise.

The whole room let out a sigh of relief! As Tim put his arm around my shoulders and gave me a quick squeeze, I lay my head on his arm feeling the relief wash over both of us.

"However," Dr. Robertson warned, his face becoming very serious again, "Nathan is going to get worse before he can get better. Actually, he is going to get very, very sick. But I am now confident that he *can* recover . . . especially because he is so young."

He went on to explain how they were able to successfully remove over half of the right lobe of Nate's liver. The downside to this was that he had to clamp off the blood supply to the whole liver again for at least thirty minutes. Unfortunately, he was not sure how the liver would react to this. "The next twenty-four to forty-eight hours are crucial!" he explained.

With tears in my eyes, I gratefully walked over and hugged Dr. Robertson. He seemed slightly surprised as I simply said, "Thank you!" After that, everyone joyfully embraced Tim and me before clearing out of the surgical waiting room.

It was then that I noticed a person sitting in the far corner where we had gathered the night before for the last rites ceremony. She was alone. I was surprised that I had not noticed her before. With family and friends scattered throughout the waiting room, I assumed that everyone was there to support Nate. I almost felt guilty that our group had been celebrating while she appeared very tired, worried, and alone. Deeply concerned, I approached her with a renewed sense of hope.

"Are you alone?" I asked softly as I sat down next to her.

"Yes," she answered wearily.

My heart went out to her as I continued. "If you don't mind me asking, who you are waiting for?"

"My fiancé is in surgery right now," she answered.

"Oh, I hope it is not too serious," I responded, realizing that it probably was this late at night.

She did not say much. Because of the compassion my friends and family had bestowed upon me, I felt an overwhelming desire to help her, especially because she was alone and in an awful state. But I was unsure how. So I offered to pray with her.

"As you probably heard the doctor say, we just had some good news concerning my son who was in a desperate situation. I am sorry that my family took over the waiting room, but we strongly believe in the power of prayer. I know the prayers of everyone gathered here tonight influenced the outcome of my son's condition. With that in mind, if you will allow it, I would like to pray for you and your fiancé," I explained.

Not even fazed by my comments, she answered, "Yes, I would like that."

So we bowed our heads. "Heavenly Father," I started as I asked God to extend the prayers that Nate had been blessed with to her and her fiancé. I continued to ask God to give both of them strength and provide healing. I finally ended it with, "In Jesus's name, amen."

She smiled and thanked me. As I walked away, I thought to myself, *Isn't it amazing how a simple gesture can affect someone else's life?*

This was a bold move for me because I usually felt uncomfortable approaching people I did not know to pray with them. I would often offer a silent prayer for people who appeared from a distance to be in distress, but that had changed for me. From that moment on, I would somehow find the courage and love to approach many strangers with very desperate circumstances during Nate's SICU stay. I noticed the same to be true for other members of my family too.

CHAPTER 12

The Resident

For the Lord is compassionate and merciful;
forgives sins and saves in time of trouble.[1]

Grateful that Nathan was finally settled in the SICU for the second time in twenty-four hours, Tim and I collapsed in the chairs next to him. It was almost 1:00 a.m. After seeing Nate, Dr. Robertson's words "very, very sick" troubled me.

I looked around the room. Nate was hooked up to even more life-support equipment. In addition to the ventilator and VAC, another large machine sat to the left, next to Nate's bed. Towering above Nate, to the right, were at least ten different medication pumps. They were divided between two different metal poles attached to stands with wheels. Each pole had two arms connected to it; one arm almost reached the top and the other sat in the middle. Our family jokingly called this setup *the tree* after one of the nurses combined the pumps onto one pole. It was quite a sight! With all of the

1. Sirach 2:11 (NABRE)

flashing lights, it reminded us of a Christmas tree. Yet the reality was that all of these medications, beeping monitors, and life-support equipment were essential in keeping this kid alive. With the situation still looking bleak, all we could do was think and live minute by minute.

By then, everyone was exhausted. After attending to Nate, a thoughtful nurse walked over to Tim and discussed possible sleeping arrangements.

"DeVos, the children's hospital connected to Butterworth, usually has a few rooms available for emergency situations like yours. I can get you a phone number if you are interested," she announced.

"Thanks! That would be nice," said Tim.

After making a few phone calls, Tim secured a room for us for the next two nights.

"Now that Nate is stable, I want you two to go get some sleep," my dad sternly insisted.

"No, I will stay with him," I started to argue.

But my dad would not hear of it. Interrupting me he said, "Michelle, you and Tim are exhausted. You both need to get some sleep."

Tim agreed, tugged on my elbow, and said, "Come on Michelle. Even if we only get a couple of hours, it will be better than sleeping in these chairs!"

Settling in the wooden chair, Mom reassured me by saying, "I promise to call if there is any change."

Dani accompanied us to the DeVos room, which was located on the twelfth floor. The rest of the kids went home with Jason and Kris. Before they left, a very thoughtful Kris said, "Here! I brought you something." She then handed me a bag stuffed with different clothes, including sweat pants, shorts, T-shirts, hoodies, and socks. She seemed to think of almost everything.

It was almost 2:00 a.m. when Tim opened the door to our room. Huge, thick windows twelve to fifteen feet high provided an incredible view of downtown Grand Rapids. It was an impressive sight for sure, with all of the tall buildings lit up in the dark night. It was like something out of a movie. I wearily stumbled to the bathroom where I found a bag of toiletries for each of us. *Ah! A toothbrush!* I thought to myself, feeling very grateful for such a small luxury. Within minutes after settling in, we were all sound asleep.

Anxious, I woke after a couple of hours sleep and hurried back to the SICU. My parents were sitting quietly among the flurry of activity when I arrived. Dad was sitting in the recliner located in the corner next to the bed. Mom had pulled the other chair close to Nate's bed and was sitting quietly holding his hand. She looked so worn out. I am sure that she had prayed most of the night while I slept. A wave of guilt washed over me knowing that she had been up all night for me; yet, I knew I absolutely needed the little sleep I received.

Dad stood up, walked over to me and gave me a hug, and then said, "Nate received some blood during the night but is still stable."

The shift nurse Emily came in. She was dressed in dark blue, as all the nurses were. She had long blonde hair that she had pulled back into a ponytail. She made her way to the right side of Nate's bed to check the multiple pumps that were beeping. After she made some adjustments and changed IV bags, she stood next to the bed. That was when I started my barrage of questions. Nate's vitals seemed to me to be on the low side again. She addressed my concerns by saying, "Things look good. Nate is stable, but I will keep a close eye on his internal pressure to avoid a repeat of yesterday."

I did not understand. I thought part of Nate's liver had been removed, so I asked, "What do you mean?"

That was when Emily briefly explained what happened. She said, "A second-year surgery resident, Dr. Fromm, saved Nate's life last night. For various reasons, pressure in his abdomen had drastically increased. Dr. Fromm recognized Nate's critical condition. Her instincts directed her to open Nate's abdomen, right here, in the room. He was immediately rushed to surgery afterward."

I was stunned! "Wow!" was all I could say. I had been praying so intently that I had not been aware of any of this.

During the time we were talking, a pretty, young blonde woman entered the room. "Here she is now," Emily said.

Dr. Fromm had a beautiful smile that lit up the room when she greeted us. She appeared to be very humble as she downplayed her role in Nate's latest emergency by saying, "I was just doing my job."

I hugged her and said, "Thank you so much." Her actions were truly brave and heroic since she had made the decision without the guidance of her supervising doctors due to an influx of emergencies.

After Dr. Fromm departed, my dad looked at my mom and said, "Come on Kathy, I am tired!" A yawn escaped him. "Let's go back to the room and get some sleep."

Mom looked at me and reluctantly said, "You call me if there is any change!"

"I will," I promised as they headed for the door.

It was approximately 8:00 a.m. when Emily entered the room again.

"The critical care team will be on rounds soon," she said.

"Thanks!" I replied and made my way to the doorway.

Rounds simply meant that the SICU team would be in to assess Nate's condition. This team usually consisted of many interns, doctors from different specialties, a pharmacist, an attending doctor, and an SICU nurse. Most of the information that the assembled team discussed was difficult for me to understand. It involved lab results, medications, ventilator data, and so on.

One thing I did find out was that from 7:00 p.m. Sunday evening until 7:30 a.m. Monday, Nate had received a tremendous amount of blood products for the third time since the accident. In this short time span, he was given twenty-two units of packed red blood cells, sixteen packs of fresh, frozen plasma, and seven five-pack platelets.

After the team departed, I continued to ask Emily numerous questions. Hearing our discussion, the attending doctor, Dr. Spencer, decided she would come back after she finished rounds with her other patients to address my concerns.

Tim and Dani made their entrance just before Dr. Spencer returned later that morning as promised. When she walked into the room, Dr. Spencer looked very serious as she summarized the latest emergency.

"Last night Nate suffered from abdominal compartment syndrome, a condition characteristic under such circumstances. It was most likely caused by blood that had gradually accumulated in his abdomen but was not able to be suctioned out properly by the VAC dressing. As this pressure increased, the blood flow to the heart became limited causing instability in his cardiovascular system. Realizing this, Dr. Fromm made a drastic call to open Nate's abdomen in the SICU room to eliminate the immediate life-threating pressure," she explained.

"So that was what I saw," Tim interrupted. "I wondered what was going on. Dr. Fromm really did open Nate up in the SICU."

Dr. Spencer continued, "Yes, and then Dr. Rodriguez came in and took over. Nate was then rushed to the OR after another massive blood transfusion. Dr. Robertson quickly joined Dr. Rodriguez. Both decided to remove a major portion of the liver's right lobe, which was dying, in order to control the main source of bleeding."

"So what is this?" I asked, pointing to the large machine next to Nate's feet?"

"During this new development, his kidneys were injured; therefore, Nate has been placed on dialysis to prevent further damage and allow his kidneys to rest," Dr. Spencer replied. "Given time, I am hopeful that his kidneys can recover from the latest trauma." Again she made it very clear that Nate was very sick. "Truly, the only thing Nathan has going for him right now is that he has not developed an infection! The next twenty-four hours will be imperative in determining whether the liver can even recover from Sunday's late-night surgery. He is nowhere close to being out of danger."

The liver provides the body with many important functions such as digestion, blood clotting, blood filtering, and the storage of various vitamins and minerals. Since the liver does so many jobs, it can be monitored by various laboratory tests. The doctors were closely watching this information. The odds, nevertheless, were still heavily stacked against Nate for many reasons. One third of his liver had been removed. The remaining portion had been compromised from coils. The Pringle maneuver blocked its entire blood flow several times within twenty-four hours. Finally, Nate had received numerous massive blood transfusions. With all of these factors against him, it would take a miracle for this cowboy to recover!

Dr. Spencer answered a few more questions, shook our hands, and left.

So we went from feeling confident after Dr. Robertson's earlier report to being very uneasy after receiving the somber news from the critical care team. This was the team responsible for monitoring everything else, not just his liver. From that moment on, we felt like we were living on a roller coaster. One moment we were celebrating good news from Dr. Robertson, who always seemed hopeful, and the next we were holding our breath with the critical care team, whose job was to remind us what enormous obstacles Nate faced.

By mid-morning, various doctors had started coming to see how Nate fared through the night. Nate had remained relatively stable compared to the day before. Many were pleasantly surprised by how well he was doing, even though he was still so critical. Dr. Rodriguez was among the influx of doctors. Again, he did not hesitate to tell us how lucky Nate was.

"He is young; he has youth on his side," he reassured us.

Dr. Robertson also checked on Nate. When he entered the room, his face beamed with optimism. He explained that he decided to leave Nate's abdomen open to ward off more pressure issues. "Now for the good news! Regardless of his physical appearance, Nate's latest blood work and liver tests show some encouraging signs that he is turning a corner," he informed us. This was great news, but, boy, did Nate look rough!

The confidence Dr. Robertson displayed when discussing Nate's condition was vital to our ability to remain positive, especially as I continued to watch Nate's blood pressure trend up and then down throughout the day. The highs and lows that the situation played on our emotions were exhausting! Although his lab reports were improving, Nate was still receiving quite a bit of blood and blood products.

Dr. Robertson made another announcement. "The latest CT scan shows that some of the packs that were used to stop Nate's internal bleeding were left in his abdomen during the last surgery. This is not surprising. Nate was so critical that we did not have the usual time to carefully count the laparotomy pads as we normally would. We rely on X-ray confirmation in these situations to make sure none are left behind." He continued to explain that Nate would still need multiple surgeries to remove the pads, wash out his wound, and finally to close the abdomen. With a smile, Dr. Robertson emphasized, "I am comfortable with the progress Nate has made and am sure he can pull through this."

Tim shook Dr. Robertson's hand and said, "Thanks for the good news."

As the day dragged on, many family members and friends

continued to visit, including Dean and the gang. Because we would gather around Nate and jokingly tell stories, a member of the critical care team pulled Tim and me into a quiet corner to remind us how serious Nate's condition was. "Nate's condition continues to be very grave," he said. "He is still very, very, very sick!" They were clearly afraid that we did not fully comprehend the seriousness of Nate's condition.

"We understand," Tim responded. "But this is how we handle serious problems. Our family jokes, laughs, and smiles as much as we can."

I secretly hoped that by hearing all of the laughter and the voices, especially of his friends, Nathan would subconsciously will himself to live.

Among the visitors were Jesse Pagtalunan and Kirsten Fortier and her three sons: Keagan, Auden, and Isaac. We had been close friends with the Fortiers for a long time. Over the years, we were very active in various activities, such as homeschool co-ops, Cub Scouts, Boy Scouts, and church youth group gatherings. Needless to say, Nate and Auden considered each other brothers.

When I met the Fortiers in the waiting room, the boys were anxious to visit Nate. Since the doctors recently reminded our family that only a few people could visit at a time, I led Keagan and Isaac through the hallway to the end of the SICU unit where Nate's room was located.

While guiding them, I tried to describe what they were about to see. Unfortunately, this was just something that could not be grasped. They were stunned when they entered the room. Tubes were everywhere! Again, Nate was so swollen that it was unsettling to look at him. In addition, he was beginning to have a yellow glow due to the buildup of bilirubin in his system. Despite this, the boys encouraged their friend to stay strong and keep fighting.

After about fifteen minutes, the two headed back to the waiting room, and I led Auden, Jesse, and Kirsten into the SICU. I again encouraged the boys to talk to their lifeless friend even though it was uncomfortable to talk to someone who could not respond. Soon Auden, with his charisma, and Jesse, with his sense of humor, began to share memories of the various antics the three boys partook in, especially at scout camp. Now with the boys more comfortable, Kirsten and I stood off to the side and quietly discussed all that had happened.

Kirsten said, "I am having a hard time grasping the fact that he was opened, packed, and shipped from Alma."

"I know," I told her. "It has all been crazy! It is hard to wrap my head around!"

"By the way, the medication stand does indeed look like a Christmas tree," she chuckled after I explained some of the life-saving equipment surrounding Nate.

Our discussion was interrupted by the nurse. "I just wanted you to know that Nate's blood pressure medications had to be increased," she said.

This was not good news to be sure! With this information, we promptly returned to the lobby where there was a rather large assembly of adults and teenagers standing and talking quietly. I asked the group if they would come together to pray since there had been a change in Nate's condition. Naturally, Aunt Shirley volunteered to lead as everyone held hands and formed a large circle. It was a good thing we held hands, for just a few words into it, Isaac's face became ghostly white and then, he fainted! Thankfully Keagan was standing next to him and helped him land softly onto a nearby couch. By the time we finished praying, Isaac had recovered.

Being the perceptive person that she was, Kirsten had brought markers and poster boards. She handed the materials over to Dani as she suggested that the teens make posters for Nate's room. It was a great idea, and even the guys participated as more than a dozen teenagers sprawled out onto the lobby floor showing off their artistic abilities. The group took up half of the waiting room. It was quite a sight. All the kids—Dani, Nick, Mathew, Andrew, cousins Brooke and Andrea, and a multitude of friends—were all pulling for Nate. It was a tender scene for Tim and me as they sat there on the floor telling funny stories about Nate while finishing up their posters. Later that evening, some of the hospital staff mentioned to me how they were touched by all the love and support Nate had received from so many people.

Up until this point, Dani, Tim, Mom, and I had been texting and calling people with updates. Since we had a large family, Dani decided to start a Facebook page titled "Stay Strong Nate." It was originally intended for our family and close friends, but in just a few hours, we received so many messages of prayers and good wishes from not only family and friends but also strangers. Tim, Dani, and I were dumbfounded.

Incidentally, just before Dani had created the page, I, in a moment of weakness, confessed to Dani that I was afraid people would assume Nate's situation had improved after the last surgery and forget to pray for him. Dani hugged me and said, "No way, Mom. There are tons of people already praying, and they won't stop!"

This proved to be true later that evening when a group of kids from Clare, including Dean who had finally gone home for a few days, organized a candlelight prayer service at the city park. More than seventy-five people attended. What was amazing to me was the unity and support our homeschooled teenager had generated throughout the local communities and on Facebook. Who could have known? Many people who could not physically attend the service joined efforts by lighting candles and praying from their homes.

A few of the many Facebook comments we received included:

"Lighting candle for Nate at 9:30 and . . . saying our prayers."

"7:30 our time here in Colorado. We will be there in spirit and prayer."

"Prayers at 9:30 from Plainwell."

"I cannot be there but I will light a candle at the same time . . . My heart goes out to the whole family."

Later in the evening when Dani and Tim sat quietly in the SICU room, Nate, for the first time, seemed to respond to their conversation with very slight facial and arm movements. When questioned about this, the nurse seemed to think that it was possible that Nate was trying to purposefully move. It was cause for another celebration!

Was this movement a figment of our imagination? Maybe or maybe not! Regardless, our family believed without a doubt that so many people's prayers were greatly impacting Nathan's condition.

Chapter 13

The Promise

Woe to timid hearts and drooping hands,
to the sinner who walks a double path.[1]

W e grew tired as the evening rolled on. "I want to sit with Nate for the first shift tonight," Dani volunteered. Tim and I were too tired to argue. We headed back to the DeVos room. It would be our last night there. Earlier in the day we had received word that a room would be available for us to relocate to the Renucci House on Tuesday.

The Renucci House was attached to Butterworth Hospital. The layout was similar to that of a hotel with many floors and rooms, except the main level had a community kitchen. People were allowed to label and store their own food in both the cupboards and refrigerator. Many times during our stay, families or organizations would generously come in and cook a free dinner for anyone staying at the house. Most of these volunteers were people who had relied on this service themselves when facing their own tragedies such as cancer,

---

1. Sirach 2:12 (NABRE)

premature births, heart attacks, car accidents, and so on.

Though I was able to sleep soundly in a comfortable bed, my motherly instinct would only allow a few hours of sleep at a time. After showering, dressing, and repacking the few bags I had for the eventual move, I quietly let myself out so I did not wake Tim and then hurried off to relieve Dani.

When I made my way back to the SICU, I found Dani fast asleep with her chair pulled up next to Nate in the darkened room. Her head was lying atop of her crossed arms on the bed next to Nate's arm; it was a heartwarming moment. I gently nudged her. "Dani, I am here. You should go back to the room and get some comfortable sleep," I said softly.

"Okay," she said, still half asleep. She gave me a hug and groggily walked out of the room.

Before I settled into the reclining chair next to Nate, I stood next to the bed and held his hand. Worry descended upon me once more so I started to pray. I asked God to allow the healing angel, Saint Raphael, to come and anoint Nate. I then touched the Fatima medal that was always taped to the head of the bed. I asked Mary to continue to intercede and plead before her son to heal my son. I would often pray this way throughout the day for the duration of Nathan's stay in the hospital.

For the next few hours I sat quietly in the dark, watching the monitors. Nathan continued to rest peacefully. Sitting there, mesmerized by the constant beeping, I realized that I had not updated the Facebook page as Dani had requested the night before. So, with my iPad in hand, I posted the following message:

As of 5:00 a.m. Tuesday, Nate seems to be taking some very small but strong baby steps in a positive direction . . . the [doctors] are very pleased. Again, I cannot stress enough what a huge hill we have to climb yet, but the [pediatric] doctor feels that he has turned the corner from existing to healing . . . He is also showing us some purposeful movements. He was trying to turn his head to my voice. I think all those who visited him yesterday were instrumental in getting him to that point.

At about 6:00 a.m. on Tuesday, activity in Nate's room slowly increased. That was about the time that Darla Nickels arrived. I was pleasantly surprised that she came so early since she lived over an hour away. It was good to see her.

Darla was a little taller than me and few years older too. Her straight, dark hair fell to her shoulders. She had a beautiful smile as she quietly entered the room. She gave me a warm hug and then we sat down and started chatting, anxious to catch up. Suddenly, all sleepiness left me as Darla reminded me that she had something important to share.

"Here it is," she said, as she handed me the little green daily devotional book titled *One Bread, One Body*. "This is what I told you about over the phone Sunday night." Taking the book, I noticed her eager expression as I began to read the following passage dated August 9, 2014, the day of the accident:

"HOW LONG, O LORD?" (PS 13:2)
IT "WILL NOT DISAPPOINT." —HABAKKUK 2:3

"Hope deferred makes the heart sick" (Prv 13:12). It is so difficult to sometimes have to wait so long for God's plan to unfold. Did you ever feel that you might die before the situation improves? Yet "the Lord does not delay in keeping His promise — though some consider it 'delay'" (2 Pt 3:9). "If it delays, wait for it, it will surely come, it will not be late" (Hab 2:3).

How do we wait for something we need so badly,

something we know for certain is God's will, and something that we just can't live another day without? We must wait patiently and confidently, not complaining. To do otherwise would be to insult God by displaying a lack of faith in His ability to deliver. We renew our strength by "waiting" upon the Lord (Is 40:31, KJV).

The Hebrew word translated as "wait" or "hope" in Isaiah 40:31 can mean to twist together, as cords of a rope are intertwined. In our waiting, then, we wrap ourselves around the Lord and He wraps Himself around us. When discouraging forces pull at us, we are not pulled apart. Instead, like strands of a rope, we and the Lord are pulled more tightly together and grow in strength. We never "come to the end of our rope" because the Lord has roped us tightly into His presence.

"Hence do not grow despondent or abandon the struggle" (Heb 12:3). Stay focused on Jesus (Heb 12:2) and confident in Him. Don't even move an inch out of your position of hope. "Look out that you yourselves do not lose what you have worked for; you must receive your reward in full" (2 Jn 8).

Prayer: Father, I will be still and know that You are God (Ps 46:11). I will hope in silence for Your saving help (Lam 3:26).

Promise: "Jesus reprimanded him, and the demon came out of him. That very moment the boy was cured"— Mt 17:18.[2]

To say I was astonished was an understatement. The whole reflection seemed to be written about Nathan's situation. I reread the passage again, amazed how accurately the words described the emotions that had engulfed my family over the last forty-eight-plus hours. And then, there

2. (Editorial Staff 2014)

it was again. I could not believe it! For a second time, God spoke to me through two very close friends. "I will be still and know that you are God." The whole passage, especially the prayer listed in that reflection, reassured me that God was with Nathan and carrying us through this uncertain ordeal. And then there was the promise. Did I dare to have trust in the words *the boy was cured*? Once again I was blessed with hope!

After I contemplated this revelation, Darla took her rosary from her pocket and joyfully said, "Let's pray." We both sat quietly in our chairs and meditated on the glorious mysteries of the Rosary, thanking God at the same time for all he had accomplished through Nathan, the medical teams, our family, and friends.

By the time we finished, the doctors were assembling in the hallway. I had not realized it earlier, but the SICU team usually started rounds with the sickest patient on the floor. And just like the two days prior, they gathered around Nate's room very early.

I stood outside as the team provided an update on Nate's current condition and the goals they hoped to see by the end of the day. They discussed the different tests he would need and identified what medications he was on and if changes needed to be made. According to the nurse's notes, albeit his blood pressure seemed to be better, he was still receiving blood products because it continued to erratically trend downward at times. He had received one unit of packed red blood cells, two units of fresh, frozen plasma, and two five-pack platelets overnight. These were improvements for sure.

One of the medications he had been on was epinephrine. Jeff Bates, who had been a pharmacist for twenty-plus years, explained to Tim and me that this was the "jet fuel" of blood pressure medication. This information did not sit very well with me as I wondered what type of side effects Nate might have to face in the future. But I knew I could not dwell on that. Despite the fact that our family's motto of living minute by minute had turned into hour by hour, I still could not allow myself to think too far into the future.

Wrapping up rounds, one of the critical care team members explained Nate's current condition with this analogy, "On Sunday night, it was as if Nate was walking on a string between life and death. On Monday, it was as if he was walking on a wire. Today Nate seemed to be on a two-by-two." So, although his condition was very serious, it appeared as if Nate's situation was slowly heading in the right direction.

Tim joined Darla and me later in the morning. Others continued to visit as well. My mom's sisters, Aunt Pat and Aunt MaryAnn, along with their husbands came to see Nate. Both of my aunts had been nurses for many years. They stayed and visited with Mom for quite some time. When they were preparing to leave, they handed me a card as I escorted them to the elevators in the waiting room. It was a generous amount of cash. I started to tell them that I could not accept such an offer, but they would not hear of it. They asserted, "It is a gift from our families. You need it after staying here this long."

Tears came to my eyes as I hugged them and graciously said, "Thank You! The only thing I ever asked anyone for was prayer."

Later that day, we found out that people back home began dropping off food at Bryan and Kelli's house for us. I think there were three coolers and a few large totes full of food. Dani had informed me that neighbors were looking after our house and animals. A cousin mowed our lawn. Friends cleaned the house and offered to can green beans and tomatoes from my garden. I was overwhelmed by all the thoughtfulness. Again, the spirit of God's charity surrounded us through the actions of so many people. I kept thinking, *How can we ever repay people?*

This goodwill, coupled with Nate's slight progress, helped our family breathe easier, and we received more good news by the end of the day. Nate had only needed four units of fresh, frozen plasma and one five-pack of platelets. His need for blood products continued to diminish along with his blood pressure medications. The doctors were finally able to eliminate the epinephrine pump, while reducing the two other blood pressure medication doses by more than half. All were good signs that his body was starting to hold its own.

CHAPTER 14

The Preparation

Woe to the faint of heart! For they do not trust,
and therefore have no shelter![1]

Nate had a pretty uneventful night. Darla joined me for the morning vigil on Wednesday. After saying the Rosary, we started to talk about the phone conversation we had during Sunday's emergency surgery.

"Darla," I said, "do you remember telling me to reflect on how God had prepared me for the accident?"

"Yes, I do," she replied, smiling confidently.

"Well, I thought about the events a few weeks prior and now realize how God had done just that," I continued.

"Of course. God always has a plan," she said excitedly. "Tell me about it."

"During this time, God took care of my in-law's needs, provided our family with unexpected cash, and finally gave me added grace through adoration and prayer," I explained.

---

1. Sirach 2:13 (NABRE)

My mother-in-law, Judi Davis, was one of my heroes. She could literally do anything, from decorating to cooking, canning, sewing, or building a wooden headboard for her bed. Not only that, but this woman attended to everyone's needs, whether it was with meals, birthday desserts, or babysitting. She had an uncanny ability to know what people needed, sometimes before they even realized it.

About three years earlier, she was diagnosed with progressive supranuclear palsy (PSP). It is a very slow, degenerative disease that had greatly affected Judi over the previous six months. Dani, my niece Jessica, Tim, and I were rotating shifts to ensure someone was there every night and most of the day to help Al care for her. The family began to question if we could continue to care for Judi at home even with support from hospice and a few other hired hands. It was mentally and physically wearing on all of us, especially Al, as her condition began to drastically decline.

Everyone knew that as summer came to a close and the next school year approached, we would have to address this issue and make some tough decisions. I would soon be focused on homeschooling, and Jessica was hoping to attend college that fall.

As a matter of fact, a few weeks before the infamous bull ride, Jessica had called. She was quite upset and asked me to meet with her. Since she was at Judi's house, which was just up the road, I hurriedly hung up the phone and drove to my in-laws house to see what the problem was. Jessica was having a difficult moment, and she told me she could not do this anymore. She shared that it was agonizing to watch her grandmother die so slowly.

After a few reflective minutes, I looked at her with compassion and asked, "Jessica, do you think this is the hardest thing you will ever have to do? Unfortunately, no," I continued, "God is just preparing you for the next difficult thing in your life. It is tough, I know, but we will get through this!"

The difficult day passed, and soon Al, Tim, and the rest of the family decided it was time to make arrangements for Judi to move into a nursing home. It just so happened that she was scheduled to move in on Monday, August 11, two days after the accident.

Another coincidence included the postponement of Al's surgery. He was scheduled to have hip surgery at the end of August. This would be the third surgery on the same hip, so we already knew he would need twenty-four-hour care for a few weeks afterward. But it would not happen due to a tooth infection; the doctor decided it was too risky and postponed the surgery.

About a week before the ride, another unusual event occurred. Tim came home from work very excited. He immediately went to our screened-in back porch and asked me to join him. Since it was a beautiful summer evening, he eagerly suggested we have a glass of wine as we sometimes did during the summer. I obliged. As I walked onto the porch, I handed him a glass. I started to sit down in one of our comfy reclining chairs when Tim handed me a lottery ticket.

"What is this?" I asked.

"Take a look!" he said.

As I glanced at it, my jaw dropped in surprise, but remembering that we lived in a house full of jokesters, I said, "Ha, Ha! The joke is over. That's funny!"

He shook his head and said, "It is no joke. This is real. I won $5,000 on a scratch off ticket!"

I was stunned! And then excitement set in because our refrigerator had not been working properly. We could get a new one. We were celebrating when the kids joined us.

Dani chuckled after Tim explained what had happened. "I was going to ask if I could borrow some money for college, but I better not. You only win money when you need it," she stated.

The final coincidence was an overwhelming desire for prayer. One night about two weeks before the accident, I attended Mass at St. Mary's Catholic Church in Mt. Pleasant. There was Eucharistic adoration after Mass, so I stayed. It was very peaceful as I sat silently praising Jesus. While praying, I asked Jesus, "Why this urgency for prayer? I had been feeling anxious for a few weeks and feeling a pressing desire to pray very frequently throughout the day, but I did not understand why. I initially thought it was because of Judi, yet a different answer came while praying the Rosary and meditating on Christ's life. I felt a gentle nudge to contemplate the meaning of the words *courage* and *love*. I told Jesus that I had no idea what that was supposed to mean, but I would pray for an increase of grace for these two virtues. Soon, very soon, I would understand why.

Little did I know at the time how significant each of these coincidences would be for our family; Tim and I did not have to worry about his parents, we had unplanned cash for hospital expenses, and I had more grace to get through the most difficult moments of my life while having the courage to approach total strangers and pray with them in their time of need. God did truly prepare us.

As Darla and I finished our conversation, the critical care team slowly began to gather in the hallway once again. Jess, the SICU nurse, gave us an update. "Good news!" she said. "Nate has been weaned off more medications. He is now down to just two medicine pumps."

I responded with, "The infamous medicine Christmas tree is slowly disappearing." We smiled as I moved closer to the door.

I stepped out of the room and into the hallway so that I could listen more intently to the discussion. I found out that Nate had received two five-pack platelets and two units of fresh, frozen plasma through the night. I heard the attending doctor say, "The main goal for the day was to prepare Nate for tomorrow's surgery."

His labs were still making small improvements, yet we were informed that he was still not even close to being out of the woods. Any infection could severely set Nate back. As the meeting concluded, the doctor explained, "Most people don't get that sick! He was really, really, really sick. Now he is just really sick."

In lieu of this information, Dani posted the following on the Stay Strong Nate Facebook page:

[We are] still unsure of the time of Nathan's surgery tomorrow. A little reality check from the doctor today has us once again begging to not forget him in your prayers. At this time, Nathan has a 50% chance of making it through this surgery. Though this is much higher than the weekend, the condition is very grave and if he contracts any infections, the percentage is greatly decreased. We know he is strong, and we are praying God gives Nathan the other 50% chance he needs to live.

A new afternoon brought a new batch of visitors. Among them were Al and two of his close friends, Frank Meyers and Gary Coats. Al, already an emotional wreck because of Judi's situation, was very upset to see his grandson. Seeing this, Tim changed the subject by asking him how Judi was doing at the nursing home. "Your mother is ready to come home!" Al said, as a small, affectionate smile crossed his lips. We chuckled at this news because she was so excited to go that she had insisted her bags be packed for days before she was scheduled to move. My heart went out to both of Tim's parents when I saw the stress my father-in-law was under.

After a few minutes, Tim turned his attention to Frank and Gary. "Thanks for coming with Dad," he said. "Traveling long distance is so hard on him. I really appreciate it."

"It was no problem," Gary replied. "We were glad to come."

The guys stayed for most of the afternoon as other guests streamed through to check on Nate. I was amazed at how many visitors Nate continued to receive throughout the day.

As the busy day started to wind down, Tim announced, "It is time for the Davises to have a quiet dinner together at the Renucci House."

Mom volunteered to keep watch. "Michelle, your dad and I will sit with Nathan. It is definitely time you guys had a break together," she said. Dad shook his head in agreement.

It was a typical, warm August evening, and the sun was still shining bright. As such, we decided to gather together on the patio for a home-cooked meal thanks to the kind-hearted volunteers who had provided us with a delicious spaghetti dinner. It was the first time I had stepped outside since Saturday, and I enjoyed the fresh, warm, evening air more than I had anticipated. The atmosphere was joyful and light. As we sat around the table ready to eat, Tim looked at me playfully and asked, "Why can't you cook this good?"

"Oh! It only tastes so good because it is not cafeteria food," I joked back.

Before we ate, Tim said the blessing, thanking God for his abundant generosity.

When we began to eat our salads, Nick jokingly asked, "Isn't it amazing how one homeschooled person can influence the world?"

Nick's humor touched upon a long-standing myth frequently associated with homeschooling families. It was common for our family to jest about how "unsocial" our kids were. In reality, they were far from being unsocial. We had been involved in Cub Scouts, Boy Scouts, 4-H, Jack Pine Ranchers & Farmers, community theater, softball, wrestling, football, baseball, soccer, and church youth groups over the years. Even so, Nick's statement made us reflect on the fact that there were people in at least nineteen states and seven countries praying for Nate. That was a remarkable number. Many people had even reached out to us through cards and donations.

During this reflective and heartfelt discussion, when we had almost finished eating, Mathew suddenly placed a spoon on the tip of his nose to balance it. "Look, no hands!" he exclaimed as all of us burst out laughing. We laughed until tears of joy streamed down everyone's face. This was truly a typical Davis family dinner moment!

After the enjoyable dinner, Dani insisted on staying with Nate again throughout the night. She was almost as reluctant to leave his side as I was. So late in the evening when all had calmed down, Tim and I went back to the room at the Renucci House while all of the kids stayed with Nate.

I woke up in the middle of the night as usual and went to relieve the Davis children. The nurse on staff that night was named Tyler, and, to pass the time, I asked him a few questions about his career. As he told me a little bit about himself, I found him to be extraordinary, very kind, patient, and sympathetic, especially as my list of questions continued. By then, my family had bestowed the title Question Queen upon me.

"Your family is awesome! It is great to see such a family pulling for Nate," Tyler commented during our conversation.

"Why thank you!" I responded, very surprised by his thoughtful remark.

"You know, families like yours bring out the best in the staff," he continued. "Many times patients' families are demanding and, unfortunately, a few are even rude . . . most likely due to the emotion and stress from their situations. But your family has been different. Their hope and cheerfulness simply changes the atmosphere in the SICU."

"What a compliment!" I said, truly humbled by his kind words. "You have not seen us on our off days though.

Maybe tomorrow," I joked.

"Well, I am sorry to say that won't happen. This will be my last night at Butterworth," Tyler added. "I am preparing for a new chapter in my nursing career."

"I am sad to hear this because you are a great nurse, yet I am very happy for the opportunities that lie before you," I replied. "I am sure you will be great at whatever you do."

As Tyler left, I thought about his words. From some of the complements I had received from many staff members, I began to wonder if our family really was unusual! I always assumed that most families were as close as ours. Tyler's comments made me appreciate our blessings even more.

At 7:00 a.m., Tyler completed his last shift with Butterworth's critical care. Before he left, I thanked him for all he had done to help Nate over the last few days and told him that he would always be in our prayers. He said thanks and wished us well as he walked out the door.

It was Thursday, surgery day! The day we had been anxiously waiting for was finally upon us. Dr. Robertson would not only remove the extra sponges but also personally see how Nate's body was reacting. Was it healing properly? Were there other issues looming? We would soon know the answers.

While we waited patiently most of the morning, various people offered their support on Facebook. Some encouraging words included:

Dear Lord. Our Almighty Physician. We pray to you to give the Davis/Cassidy family hope . . . love . . . and courage. Be with them during this time and give them faith knowing you are in that operating room guiding the Dr.'s hands and whispering words of strength and comfort to Nate. Amen. Praying for you all! Stay strong Nate.

—Dawn Swartzmiller

I offered the Mass for Nathan this morning. We all will be praying for him and his doctors this afternoon.

—Deb McGraw

Father you are the creator of all life and we ask that you protect Nathan's life thru this surgery. Father be with Tim and Michelle, give them comfort and peace and wipe away all their fears. Thru this trial we ask that they would have joy in Jesus Christ. Protect Nathan from complications or infections. We rejoice together on what you have done and what you are continuing to do in Nathan's healing and recovery. In the powerful name of Jesus Christ. Amen.

—Jody Yates Best

In preparation for the big event, my sister-in-law Kris surprised us while in Nate's room by handing out T-shirts to the Davis clan.

"What are these for?" Nick questioned, as a smile broke out on his face when he realized each represented a Marvel or DC comic book superhero.

"Well, the kids, Jason, and I thought it would be great to show some *superhero support* today," she said. "Brandon and Emma already have theirs on."

This enthusiasm caught on because the next thing I knew, Mom, Dad, Steve, Bryan and Kelli and their kids, Brooke, Eric, Kyle, and Jake all had superhero shirts on. Friends and extended family arrived wearing them too. It was a bit of comic relief amid such seriousness. We were quite a sight to be sure as superheroes such as Batman, Superman, and Captain America filled the waiting room.

Several staff members commented each time a new superhero entered. "What a great idea!" one said. The others nodded in agreement.

The shirts had a superhero picture on the front and my favorite Bible verse, "Be still and know that I am God" handwritten on the back. It attracted so much attention that numerous strangers in the SICU family waiting room questioned the occasion also.

When Nathan was finally wheeled out of the SICU room, family and friends again gathered in the surgical waiting room as they had the first two days of our journey. The atmosphere was light and assured, not nearly as nerve racking as with the previous surgeries. As usual, everyone intuitively gathered around, held hands, and prayed. The prayer we selected came from a Facebook post that our friend Debbie sent earlier that morning. Dani led us in prayer:

> Holy Father, we ask that your hands guide the hands of Nate's surgeons, and ask Jesus, the healer of all healers, to put his hands on Nate and heal him completely and wholly. Father, I ask that you send your Holy Spirit to be with Tim and Michelle and the kids right now that they may be comforted and know your peace. Remove any anxiety or fear from their minds and hearts, and let them rest in the knowledge that You are present.

> Prepare the surgical room to be a place of peace. Touch and bless the surgeon and the surgical staff. May their minds be alert and their hands skillful. Lead them as they attend to routine or unfamiliar tasks.

> Hold Nate in your hands through the entire procedure. May the events of this day contribute to his healing, and may the best be done according to your wisdom and love. Amen.

Afterward, everyone settled in, and the smiling and joking

began. Aside from the fact that some uncertainty lingered, a strong feeling of confidence remained amongst us.

Unlike after the previous surgeries, Dr. Robertson soon appeared in the doorway. Dressed in his usual baby blue, he had a big smile on his face. He joyfully looked to Tim and announced, "Everything went well!" Dr. Robertson then motioned for Tim and me to join him in one of the smaller conference rooms.

As he ushered us in, Dr. Robertson did not expect to see a large influx of family members fill in behind us. Still smiling, Dr. Robertson patiently waited as we crowded into the tiny room. Once everyone was situated, Dr. Robertson began to recap where Nate was physically and what to expect next. He took his time while recounting all the details of the surgeries Nate had thus far. He emphasized each step: removing the missed packs, washing out Nate's abdomen, and, finally, further inspecting Nate's liver and intestines.

"Except for the scar tissue that will form, everything else looks great and I am extremely pleased," he announced. "It does not appear as though Nate had trauma to any other organs, which is very remarkable."

The enthusiasm in the room grew as Dr. Robertson continued, "I expect some issues like fevers to occur, but at the moment, good progress has been made."

Dr. Robertson went on to warn Tim and me that with situations like this, problems can occur when trying to stretch the abdominal skin enough to permanently close the wound. After explaining this process in more detail, he announced, "In order to prevent further abdominal pressure and eventually close the wound, I decided that Nate's abdomen should be temporarily closed with Velcro. This Velcro patch will be slowly tightened until the wound can be permanently closed with staples and stitches."

With this news, as if on cue, my dad, Tim, and brothers looked at each other and jokingly expressed interest in Velcro for their "belly issues" too. My dad voiced what all of them were thinking. "If this Velcro idea is considered for a weight loss plan, we would like to be added to the test group," he said, rubbing his own belly.

Dr. Robertson chuckled as laughter filled the room. Then he continued, "Unfortunately, I will not be able to perform the next surgery because I will be out of town. A colleague of mine will be caring for Nate. Don't worry though, the next surgery will be simple, and I do not expect any issues."

After all the good news, Tim and my brothers shook Dr. Robertson's hand. As I approached, he looked at me and jokingly said, "Are you going to hug me again?" Everyone laughed!

I said, "Of course! If you do not mind!"

He smiled and warmly said, "I welcome it."

Our little crowd made their way to the waiting room while Tim relayed the information to those who could not join us. As everyone breathed a huge sigh of relief, Tim and I turned and embraced each other with the biggest bear hug ever! Peace immediately filled the room. Thankfully, God was still smiling upon us.

Once Nate returned from surgery to the SICU, several visitors popped in to check on him. My niece Emma was among them. As she started toward him, she suddenly fell to the floor. She had fainted. Because she had visited Nate many times her reaction came as a surprise to everyone.

A few minutes after she had recovered, Andrew nonchalantly stated, "Emma, don't be afraid of the puffiness!" Laughter ensued.

The rest of the evening was uneventful, which was just what we had hoped for.

Rounds did not occur until later on Friday morning. It was nearly 10:30 p.m. by the time the team finally assembled. The attending doctor reviewed Nate's charts and appeared very positive. He felt that Nate was doing well except for a few issues concerning slightly elevated muscle enzymes. Again, there were some concern about abdominal compartmental syndrome so the team would continue to monitor Nate closely. The best news, however, was that Nate had remained stable since the procedure the day before without needing additional blood pressure medication.

The attending doctor looked at me and said, "I am going out on a limb here, but I think his kidneys are going to recover just fine." This was more good news! *Oh . . . the power of prayer* was all I could think.

Since Nate's progress was consistent, the next issue, brain functionality, was lingering in the back of each doctor's mind. Being a nursing student, Dani had already pointed out that aside from the small signs of purposeful movements such as opening his eyes, brain damage was a serious concern because of how very critical Nate had been. He had lost so much blood, especially before he even made it to Gratiot Medical Center in Alma. Nate's surgeon in Alma would later tell us how, based on the fact that Nate went blind after stumbling off the arena, he must have gone nearly ten minutes without much blood to his brain; brain damage can happen in less than four minutes!

Although I felt that this concern was downplayed by the staff for our sake, I could tell from the current conversation that the team was paying more attention to the rest of Nate's body because he was more stable from his liver injury. The team discussed a possible fracture to Nate's neck, but a more in-depth examination indicated that it was from an older injury.

In an attempt to lighten up the serious atmosphere, the attending doctor announced, "We will truly know if Nate has brain damage if he ever gets on a bull again."

Without realizing the humor in his remark, I anxiously shook my head and started to explain that no one would let that happen, but I suddenly realized that he was just joking.

I smiled sheepishly as everyone else chuckled at my inability to recognize the joke. It was a wonderful moment because it was evidence that the critical care team was more confident in Nate's ability to recover.

Tim joined me sometime after rounds and not long after that Dr. Robertson came in. His face beamed with a grand smile from ear to ear.

Dr. Robertson's enthusiasm was catchy as Tim smiled back and stated, "When the doctor smiles, we smile!"

"Nate's liver lab data looks great! His liver is now working!" Dr. Robertson announced. Not wanting to give us the wrong impression, he cautiously continued, "Still, it will be a long haul, but I think we are past the touch-and-go phase!" Tim and I breathed a huge sigh of relief as he said, "The kidneys appear to be working just fine on dialysis. I expect them to make a full recovery as well." Nodding his head, he said confidently, "It could be three days, three weeks, or a few months, but I think they—the kidneys—are coming back!"

"Praise God!" was all we could say.

Then he told us some more good news. "I have rearranged my schedule so that I can perform the next surgery after all."

This change of plans was very exciting news for us since we were partial to Dr. Robertson by now. Not that we doubted any other doctor's abilities, but our family felt such a strong bond for this man that it was difficult to think anyone else could do the job better.

"I will schedule a surgery for Friday to wash out Nate's abdomen, check his liver, and tighten the Velcro," he explained, assuming the wound would not be ready to close permanently.

After answering a few questions, Dr. Robertson shook Tim's hand and prepared to leave.

Later that day, Nate really struggled after the critical care team decided that it was time to reduce the sedation and pain medications to see how he would respond. Nate was so restless that the staff had to strap down his arms so that his movements did not interfere with all of his IVs. Needless to say, we were all surprised and very excited when Nate tried to communicate by nodding his head or shaking it to indicate yes or no when questioned.

Tim asked Nate, "Can you hear me?" Nate slowly motioned in what appeared to be a nod. Not quite sure of the response, Tim asked, "Was that a 'yes'?" Again, Nate appeared to nod his head. We were ecstatic. But as the day continued, the pain became too great, and an increase in the sedation and pain medications was necessary to allow Nate to rest comfortably.

CHAPTER 15

The Dream

Woe to you that have lost hope!
What will you do at the Lord's visitation?[1]

Nate made it a whole week! I thought. Friday, August 15, blended into Saturday, marking one week since tragedy and struck our family. We had finally progressed from looking at life hour by hour to day by day. Nate had endured six critical surgeries in seven days. The trials and miracles our family witnessed leading up to our one-week milestone were pretty unbelievable.

As I was thinking about all of this, a stranger entered the room surprising Tim and me. He had blond hair that peaked out from under his cowboy hat. He had a warm smile as he introduced himself. "Hi, I am Aaron Young," he stated, as he extended his hand in a friendly handshake.

"Finally we meet," Tim said.

Aaron was a fellow bull rider who had been helping Nate train. He was married and had two children. Nate loved

1. Sirach 2:14 (NABRE)

141

Aaron's kids and talked about the Young family often. Nate would go over to Aaron's to practice riding on barrels almost every day after work. Although Aaron was a few years older than Nate, they had formed a solid friendship. Aaron had been riding for quite some time and had experienced a few injuries, but on no occasion had he sustained a severe one.

Aaron was deeply concerned for his younger friend as he approached Nate's bed. Nate seemed to smile when he saw him, and Aaron stayed for a while to keep Nate company. As his visit came to a close, Aaron asked if there was anything he could do for us. We thanked him and assured him that we had plenty of help. Aaron continued to keep in close contact with us, checking in to see if we needed help at the homestead and visiting his friend often.

In between visitors, Nate was whisked away for yet another surgery. "Everything seems to be healing well, and I was able to tighten the Velcro." Dr. Robertson informed us. "Also, I am hopeful that we will be able to completely close the wound in a couple of days."

While monitoring Nate postsurgery, the nurse reminded us that Nate continued to take baby steps that were "trending in the right direction," and by Sunday, Nate's labs looked strong. We were informed after rounds that his liver seemed to be mending so well that the critical care staff finally mentioned the next milestone, nutrition. Although he was not quite ready for it, the fact that the critical care team was discussing it was cause for celebration. It meant that the team was focused on Nate's future needs rather than just his immediate needs.

It was truly a rare event for the Davis family to miss a weekend Mass. Since Nate was doing better and my parents were keeping him company, Tim, Dani, and I decided to walk to St. Patrick's Cathedral late Sunday morning. Pat Cook, taking his godfather duties seriously, had thoughtfully made sure Nick (his godson), Mathew, and Andrew went to church the night before. After church, Pat treated the trio to ice cream at the local Dairy Queen, making it a very enjoyable break from the hospital scene.

The cathedral was only a few blocks away. It was another beautiful, sunny day. As we crossed the road, I wondered if the accident had forced me to recognize beautiful days instead of taking them for granted. Each day since we arrived at the hospital seemed pristine. I especially took pleasure in feeling the warm rays on my face. Who could not help but smile on such a bright, sunny day? Even though I enjoyed being outside, Nate was never far from my thoughts.

Dani distracted my thoughts with a peculiar story. She told me that while they were at Michelle and Jeff's house in Minnesota, just a day before the accident, Caley Meixner had a dream. She said, "At first it did not seem too important, but now . . . well . . . you decide." Kent, a close friend of Caley who had passed away a few months earlier, appeared to her in a dream. After some discussion, Kent urgently stressed to Caley, "No matter what happens, everything will be all right." When she woke up, Caley, puzzled by the experience, wondered "What did this mean? What would be all right?"

"Mom," Dani clarified, "we just shrugged it off."

I immediately had goosebumps. Was Kent referring to Nathan?

"Isn't that crazy?" Dani asked.

While we continued to walk, I thought about the dream. Was this yet another coincidence or, as I started calling them, "God moments," like those I had discussed with Darla earlier in the week? Anything seemed possible at that point.

After church services, the three of us quickly walked back to the hospital. Soon after, more visitors came, including many from the rodeo circuit. Caleb Wilson, Elizabeth Elaine, and Tanner Ruby and his sister Kirsten gathered in Nate's room. Someone started to talk about riding in Saturday's upcoming rodeo. As the conversation continued, Nate became agitated.

He was starting to open his eyes more by that time and it seemed as if he was trying to tell us something by the way he moved his eyes back and forth.

After observing his actions, Kristin said, "Nate seems interested in riding in the next rodeo."

Nate nodded ever so slightly while trying to move his lips. Tim and I were stunned for two reasons: First, because he had been listening and was communicating with us. Second, because Nate somehow thought he could ride again.

That was when Tim broke the news to him. "Nate, you have been in the hospital for over a week in a medically induced coma." Again, Nate became restless as he attempted to move his arms and legs with only a little success. Tim and I knew that Nate had originally planned to ride in the Midland County Fair, which was only a few days after the Gratiot County Fair. Tim continued to explain, "Nate, you cannot ride again. Besides, the Midland County Fair has come and gone."

Nate shook his head in disbelief.

"You have been in the hospital for over a week from a bull-riding injury in Alma. Right now all you need to worry about is getting better," Tim again reminded Nate.

With that information, Nate gave up, settled back down, and dozed off to sleep.

Sometime during our bull-riding conversation, Kelsey Barber, our next-door neighbor, and David Schwab slipped into the room. Kelly, Kelsey's mom, was with them. David was also a bull rider who had been dating Kelsey for quite some time. After Nate's unsettling interest in bull riding, I decided I needed a break from the crowded room and the conversation. I asked Kelly to join me as I made my way to the waiting room.

Over the past few years, the families from our neighborhood had seen a few misfortunes ranging from fires to cancer. For example, one May morning a couple of years earlier, Nathan called out to me that he had seen smoke coming from the Newman Family Dairy Farm, which was Kelly's parents' farm. Before I knew it, all the neighbors had bolted down the road to help out. By the time I got there, the whole wooden gable-style barn was engulfed in flames. The fire was so intense that the plastic dashboard of a truck sitting in front of the mechanical barn about one hundred and fifty feet away actually melted. Thankfully, nobody was in the barn. Burning embers floated in the air as all of us scrambled to keep the house safe. We sprayed the roof down with the garden hose until the fire department came. Little fires sprang up in the nearby field. A few people used shovels and buckets of water to extinguish them. Luckily, the fields were not very dry that day.

The barn was a total loss. Almost half of the Newman's dairy cows, their livelihood, had been wiped out! It was a sickening feeling to see the one-hundred-year-old landmark and so many animals gone. These types of events drew our little farming community together because of the sheer pain and suffering that friends and family witnessed. It bonded an already close neighborhood. So it came as no surprise that a couple of hours drive failed to keep the Barbers away from our own unfortunate circumstances.

Some of the Schunk family, Jo, Dean's mom, and his sister Alex, came after the Barbers left. Although Jo only lived a couple of miles from us, her kids were in the Clare County school district, not Beaverton. The Schunks were well known in the 4-H crowd and the Clare community and, for a homeschooled kid, Nate had many connections through his friendship with Dean.

Jo and Alex brought us a large basket of goodies: snacks, crossword puzzles, books, and other necessities like toothbrushes and hand sanitizer. It was such a thoughtful and appreciated gesture. When I guided Jo and Alex down the long hallway back to the SICU to see Nate, Jo had a hard time. Nate and Dean had become such close friends, and she felt like Nate was one of her own.

"So many people are praying!" Jo informed me as their visit drew to a close.

With confidence, I simply responded, "That is the reason Nate is still alive!"

CHAPTER 16

The Setback

Those who fear the Lord do not disobey his words;
those who love him keep his ways.[1]

Our positive baby steps came to a halt on Monday when Nate developed a fever. I seemed to face another roller coaster as I recalled Dr. Spencer warning that a fever could cause a major setback. Due to Nate's injured kidneys and liver, acetaminophen and ibuprofen were not optimal choices. Thus, that pesky knot in my stomach seemed to grow once again, even though the doctors continued to warn us about these types of problems.

To try and keep Nate's fever under control, I helped the nursing staff keep a cool cloth on his forehead while wiping his arms and legs with another. The nurses placed icepacks between his arms and chest. To keep busy, I kept them filled as they melted. When Nate's fever went above one hundred degrees, the nurses placed a cooling blanket over him.

With this new condition, Nate became more restless, and

1. Sirach 2:15 (NABRE)

he seemed to be fighting the ventilator at times. He would try to push it out of his mouth. The doctors had to secure his arms once again.

The good news returned when the medical team finally decided to feed Nathan later in the day. A feeding tube was inserted through Nate's nose down into his stomach. Everyone was relieved to see him receive nourishment at last. Still, as with all traumatic situations, there was some concern as to how Nate's body would react. We would have to wait and see.

Later in the afternoon, the Donavan family arrived. Their visit came at a perfect time, providing me with a distraction from the fever setback. Zack had been with Nate the day of the accident and was finally able to see him. As I escorted everyone to Nate's SICU room, I again tried to prepare them for what they would see. Zack and his older brother Nick were pretty quiet as they entered the room. It was truly a rare event. The boys found the courage to talk to Nate, who was finally able to communicate a little with a pen and paper.

After a few minutes, Zack's mother, Vicki, and her two daughters, Emily and Sam, escorted me back to the waiting room leaving the boys to sit with Nate. Vicki had been a constant advocate for Nate from the start. She had added Nate to her church's prayer chain right away. Their family prayed constantly, especially those first forty-eight hours.

As we sat in the waiting room visiting, Vicki expressed her gratitude for the Facebook updates. "I am so thankful that Dani created a Facebook page!" she exclaimed. "The updates make me feel as though I am partaking in your crazy roller coaster journey. Whenever Nate has a good day, I have a good day, and when Nate has a rough day, I seem to struggle too."

By early Tuesday morning, Nate's fever had crept up to over 102 degrees Fahrenheit. I knew that more aggressive measures would be needed to control his fever. *What if it could not be controlled? What other medications could be used other than acetaminophen and ibuprofen?* I thought. These were just some of the questions that struck me.

The nurse informed me that Nate would be receiving some acetaminophen to keep the fever in check.

"What about his kidneys and liver?" I asked, as if they were not already aware of the dangers.

"It is only a small amount. Hopefully that is all he will need," the nurse reassured me.

She was right. The small amount of acetaminophen, in conjunction with the cooling blanket and ice packs, kept his fever within limits. Thank God, since his next surgery was scheduled for that afternoon.

At 2:00 p.m., Nate was wheeled out of the SICU to surgery. Soon afterward Dr. Robertson came in with an update. "Nate's abdomen is finally closed," he said. "No more Velcro! Instead, he has more than fifty staples plus many internal stitches."

"Nate will always have a conversation piece with the scar he is going to have," Dr. Robertson assured us, smiling.

Everyone laughed. Dr. Robertson told us how he had rinsed out Nate's abdomen one more time and checked to make sure his liver was still mending well.

"I am very, very pleased," he said. "However, I did spy a potential problem. There are some pockets of fluid that have accumulated around the liver, which probably caused the fever. I will put him on an antibiotic right away."

"What caused the fluid buildup?" Tim asked.

"The body, ridding itself of the dead liver tissue, most likely caused the buildup," Dr. Robertson explained. "Usually the body can absorb this tissue while naturally expelling it. In this case, Nate's body has too much dead tissue, and he is having trouble eliminating it. I drained it during surgery. But, if Nate's body cannot absorb future fluid buildup, he will need either a couple of drain tubes inserted into his abdomen or another operation. The problem with the last option is that once permanently closed, the abdomen goes through a delicate healing phase. This phase can take a couple of weeks to complete. A surgery during this time can cause a greater risk of intestinal damage. Because I do not want to interfere with the healing and run that risk, surgery would only be a last resort. I am pretty confident that one or two drain tubes can take care of the problem."

Everyone quietly savored the moment. Then Dr. Robertson simply nodded his head, smiled, and stated with confidence, "He's gonna make it!"

What a miracle, considering what Nate had been through. "I will have to give you a hug after all the good news," I informed Dr. Robertson.

"I have come to expect it," he chuckled.

Once the sedation from surgery wore off, Nate was much more alert. His fever subsided as Dr. Robertson had predicted. Nate's nurse also informed us that Dr. Spencer was finally thinking about taking him off the ventilator. He had been on various sedatives, which can cause a person to forget to breathe, so the doctors explained that the weaning process would take some time and we needed to be patient. Also, his oxygen levels and positive end-expiratory pressure (PEEP) were too low; because of this, Nate would need to practice breathing while still on the ventilator. Furthermore, Dr. Spencer wanted to see a drop in fluid buildup surrounding Nate's lungs before she felt comfortable allowing him to breathe on his own. This postponement was not popular with Nate. He was so frustrated with that tube in his mouth, and I could not blame him.

That evening Tim and I stayed with Nate for the first shift. Mathew had gone home with my mom to check on our animals. Dani, Nick, and Andrew went back to the room. They planned on relieving us sometime after midnight. It was funny how tired I could get just sitting around not really doing anything. As we sat quietly, Nate started to become restless again. I moved next to the bed so I could remind him where he was and why he was here. With his eyes closed, he tried to nod his head as if to say, "Yes, yes, I know." I started to straighten out his blankets when I noticed that he was moving his lips as if to say something. I placed my hand into his partially closed fist and asked, "Nate, do you need something?"

He just squeezed my hand and ever so slightly nodded as he continued to move his lips. I still could not figure out what he was trying to say so I asked Tim, who was snoozing in his chair, for assistance.

"Can you figure out what Nate is trying to say?" I asked.

After studying Nate for a minute, Tim calmly announced, "I think he is praying the Rosary." Nate squeezed my hand again and nodded to affirm Tim's conclusion. I was surprised!

I did not expect this. "Do you want us to say it with you?" I questioned. He nodded in agreement. So Tim and I started to pray out loud as Nate quietly mouthed the words the best he could. We did not get very far into the prayer before Nate fell peacefully back to sleep.

By Wednesday morning, our family was very hopeful that Nate would be taken off the ventilator, but we were disappointed after rounds. Dr. Spencer came into the room to explain the situation.

"I do not think Nate is ready. The latest X-ray still shows more fluid around his lungs. I just am not comfortable proceeding yet. We will take another X-ray tomorrow, and I will decide then."

Despite the fact that Nate was breathing somewhat on his own, Dr. Spencer still felt his breathing needed to be stronger. In the meantime, Nate would be placed on another antibiotic to ward off pneumonia.

Tim, Nick, Dani, Andrew, and I decided to head back to the Renucci room for lunch while Nate slept soundly. Mathew was still at home with Grandma. On our way back to the

SICU after lunch, we ran into Dr. Rodriguez in the hallway that connected the Renucci House to the emergency wing. It was a pleasant surprise since we had not seen him in quite a few days.

"I have been keeping a close eye on Nathan's remarkable progress, especially after Sunday's close call due to abdominal compartmental syndrome," he reassured us.

"That was quite a night!" Tim replied.

Dr. Rodriguez continued casually, "By the time I entered the room, Dr. Fromm had already saved his life. Even though the situation was still quite serious, I was not too concerned."

"Really, why not?" Tim questioned slightly surprised.

"Well, when I walked into Nate's room, out of the corner of my eye I caught sight of something. As I turned my head toward the head of the bed, I saw your family huddled together in prayer. I knew then that Nate would be just fine," Dr. Rodriguez explained. "Now Nathan is not a Lazarus," he said, "but he is very close!"

A Lazarus is a biblical reference to the friend of Christ who Christ raised from the dead.

"Your family has a strong faith," he continued. "It was nice to see it in such a traumatic moment," he stated with a smile.

As we were about to part ways, Dr. Rodriguez turned back to us and said, "Oh, by the way! I wanted you to know that I presented Nate's case to a group of hospital vice presidents to show how well all the teams worked together. It was very impressive, from the ambulance, Gratiot Medical Center, and Spectrum Health Aero Med to the surgical and trauma care teams. Nate has had a pediatrics team, adult surgery team, a trauma unit, and critical care unit all caring for him over the past twelve days. That takes quite a bit of coordination and cooperation."

As he finished, Dr. Rodriguez revealed to us that Nate's experience would be used for many case studies, which could help save other lives. "I have a video clip of the accident, if that would be useful," Dani offered.

Dr. Rodriguez replied, "In most traumatic cases, the doctors rarely see how an injury happens, just the end result. I would gladly take a copy of the video. It would definitely help in understanding this and possibly other traumas."

Dr. Rodriguez handed us his business card as we said our goodbyes.

When we came back from lunch, we were surprised to see Nate had another visitor, Kyle Schunk. Kyle, Dean's older brother who had been with us during Nate's surgery Sunday night, stood next to Nate holding a notepad. Even though Nate was able to communicate by jotting down words on the notepad, it was very difficult to understand because of his sloppy handwriting as a result of his sedation.

"While you were gone, Nate and I had quite a talk," Kyle said shaking the notepad.

"Oh? About what?" Tim replied.

"Well, actually, we argued about how long he has been in the hospital," Kyle continued.

Tim laughed and said, "Yes, we have already had that discussion."

"Nate is convinced that he has only been unconscious for two days. To make matters more interesting, Nate wants to ride in the next fair rodeo," Kyle smirked.

We were all silent, especially in light of the conversation with Tanner last weekend. "Don't worry! I made it very clear to Nate that if he ever thinks about riding again, I would kick his butt. And then Dean would, and then Devon . . . actually, there are a lot of people who will not let him get back on a bull." Kyle reassured us after seeing the concern on all of our faces.

"Thanks Kyle," was all I could say as I stood there next to Nate's bed wondering if Nate would really leave this hospital only to try to ride again. That wretched knot in my stomach suddenly tightened again. Someone once told me that bull riding was very addictive. Nate's response seemed to support such a theory. Would Nate actually ride again? I could not understand how he could want to after all he had been through.

The rest of the day was pretty uneventful. Because of this and the fact that Nate was recovering well, Tim decided that he had better take a trip home.

"I do not want to go. I hoped to be able to see Nathan off the ventilator and hear his voice," Tim said to me. He sounded a little discouraged.

I hated to see him leave too. "Can't you stay just one more day?" I asked.

"I better not. This way I can go back to work for a few days. You know my vacation time is almost gone." Tim stated. Since he had worked at the phone company for more than twenty years, we were fortunate that he had four weeks of vacation time.

"I guess," was all I could say, trying not to be too upset. After all, what did I expect? He did have a job.

After a quick dinner, Tim packed some dirty laundry in a bag, loaded Andrew and Nick into the Ford, and headed home. It was the first time in thirteen days Tim had been home.

More progress came with a new day. By late Thursday afternoon, Nate's lab numbers were still improving, and Dr. Spencer finally gave the all-clear signal to take him off the ventilator. This was a huge physical milestone as well as a psychological one. Dani and I could hardly hear him speak. Even so, Nate was finally able to vocalize some of his thoughts instead of writing them down.

After the ventilator was removed, the nurses helped Nate sit up in bed. That was when I noticed his hair was a mess and all over the place. It made me smile because it reminded me how fast it grew. *As soon as he gets home, I will have to make an appointment with Monica to get that wild hair cut.* I thought to myself. *Home! Do I dare think of going home?* I wondered while I watched the nurses help Nate settle back into a lying position to rest. Because he was so weak, he was only able to sit for about fifteen minutes before he was physically drained. Still, it was another positive step forward.

My mom and Mathew returned later that evening. It was her birthday. After I told her about all of the wonderful progress Nate had made and she saw how alert he was, Mom announced, "This is the best present I could have asked for." Since Mathew had not seen Nate in a couple of days, he insisted on keeping Nathan company that night. Mom, who had been missing Nate, joined Mathew.

Nate had finally crossed the two-week milestone. Nevertheless, more bumps in the road came on Saturday. Nate started having serious abdominal pains and began vomiting. Nate's medical team called in a GI specialist to help properly diagnose Nate's condition. I was back on the worry roller coaster. Although he never complained, Nate was definitely tired of all the poking and prodding. He certainly was not one for much attention. It turned out that Nate had two issues: First, his sodium levels were dangerously low. Second, he suffered from intestinal lesions. Once Nate started taking sodium tablets, some of the symptoms subsided. The lesions, however, would need a couple of days to heal.

On a more exciting note, Cody Boyer from Northern Michigan's 9&10 News had prepared a small segment about Nathan at the beginning of the week. He had interviewed my parents with my brother Jason back in Gladwin a few days prior. The segment was set to air on the 6:00 p.m. and 11:00 p.m. newscasts that night. It was exciting for the Davis family because I had asked Cody to focus on thanking the community for all of the support they had shown us over the last couple of weeks.

Many people had sent us gifts. There were homemade

blankets, cards, balloons, clothes, food baskets, generous monetary donations, gas cards, room expense certificates, rosaries, and so on. Quite a few businesses in Clare had posted signs that read, "Stay Strong Nate." Other businesses had collection jars that the community generously contributed to. A few friends and our church's youth group also hosted a few bake sales in Nate's honor. Kristin Ruby gathered additional support by creating T-shirt for our local communities to wear.

We thought Kristin's T-shirts were a great idea. She had "Stay Strong Nate" printed on the front. So many people purchased them that she was able to give one to each member of my immediate and extended family. What I found most significant was the phrase she had printed on the back: "I can do all things through Christ who strengthens me" (Phil 4:13). We wore the shirts often and people would stop us and ask about the story behind it.

We were thankful to Cody and 9&10 News for giving us an opportunity to show our gratitude to those who prayed, donated, and helped in any way. Nate was moved by the news story as well. By then he was more alert and able to consistently remember what had happened, and after seeing the news segment online, he started asking about the details surrounding the accident. As the family described the events over the last few weeks and all of the community support we had received, Nate grew very quiet. "I do not deserve this," was all he could say.

On Sunday morning, Tim and the boys returned. After church, we received more good news. Super Nurse Jess, as we affectionately called her, was determined to take Nate outside. Even though I was nervous about the idea, I knew that everything would be okay because Jess seemed to have a healing touch. It seemed that whenever Nate's vital signs started to trend down, she knew just what to do, and they would perk back up again before we knew it.

As she got him ready, she looked at me and said, "Nate needs this. Going outside will be a huge boost for him mentally and emotionally." So by late morning, Jess, the IV stand, and a wheelchair-bound Nathan took a stroll out the front door of the Meijer Heart Center. Jess positioned Nate just outside the door but in the sun. Dani and Mathew helped her with the doors and the IV stand.

It was so strange to see him outside as he was very yellow. He had developed a severe case of jaundice due to his damaged liver. Dani told Nate, "You look like an Oompa Loompa from the movie *Willy Wonka and the Chocolate Factory.*" I did not realize how yellow he had become until he was in the sunlight. It was very prominent.

"Thanks," he said, as a tiny smile crossed his weary lips. We could barely hear him because his voice was still very weak.

Ten minutes of fresh air did wonders for Nate, just as Jess had predicted. Seeing that he was becoming very tired, she announced it was time to go inside and hurried us back to the SICU room. Although he did not stay outside long, Nate could mark another milestone; we had made more progress!

Since so many people were following Nate's story on Facebook, Dani posted the following simple message to remind everyone how vital their prayers had been in helping Nate get to this point:

"Nate went outside for the first time in over [two] weeks today! He did great!"

CHAPTER 17

The Strangers

Those who fear the Lord seek to please him;
those who love him are filled with his law.[1]

During Nathan's stay in the SICU, I met and talked with many strangers. These discussions were often initiated in the Surgical ICU family waiting room as the relatives of patients tried to escape their own serious family situations, if only for a few moments.

One evening, as my mom came back into Nate's room, she told me about a couple of ladies she had met in the waiting room. She encouraged me to meet them. So after Nate was settled for the night, I wandered into the waiting room. The hospital staff had dimmed the lights since it was getting late. Even though the lighting made it difficult to see, I noticed that they were sitting by the entrance making rosaries. After introducing myself, I found out that they were sisters whose mother was in the SICU. While their mother's situation appeared bleak, peace surrounded the sisters, and

I was instantly drawn into their conversation. I enjoyed our discussion and was amazed at their display of confidence in Divine Providence. They believed God knew what was best for their family and was ready to accept whatever his plan was. I kept thinking, *If only I could trust like that!*

Another difficult situation that I encountered was with the mother of a patient who had been in a serious car accident. Darla and I had met her in the SICU hallway, not long after the young man had arrived. Seeing how distraught she was, we approached her and asked if we could pray with her. She gratefully agreed. As we finished praying, I asked God to extend the blessings from those who had prayed for us to this young man. The mom was so thankful that we decided to take time to comfort her. She explained that she had a difficult relationship with her son. Darla promised her that we would keep both of them in our prayers.

Every so often, over the next week, I bumped into this woman. We gave each other updates on each son's progress and encouraged one another. One day, a nurse brought me a note. It had a room number listed along with a request. The mom stated that she had been looking for me and was hoping that I could take a minute to meet her son. As I looked up from the little note, the nurse informed me that the young man was to be discharged soon so I should hurry to find him.

When I approached the young man's room, he was sitting in a wheelchair with his leg extended. It had been severely broken but was mending well. He still looked pretty rough, but seemed anxious to leave the hospital. I introduced myself to him. He asked me if I was one of the ladies that had prayed for him. I told him I was. He said he wanted to thank me. He also said that his mom was sorry she would miss saying goodbye. After we talked for a few minutes, I wished him well. As I turned to leave, I found myself amazed once again at how taking just a few minutes to reach out to others could have such a significant impact.

One of the prayer requests we received involved premature twins. One was doing fine but the other had very serious complications and was not expected to live. Before we left the hospital, however, I learned that both would soon be homeward bound. It was truly another miracle!

Probably the most profound encounter I had at the hospital was with a woman named Danette. She stood about five feet four inches tall with long, dark hair and a gentle smile. Danette cautiously approached me in the waiting room one late afternoon during the middle of Nate's second week and said, "I have watched your family over the past week. It appears as though your situation is getting better."

"Yes," I told her, grateful for her kindness. "Things seem to be moving in the right direction by the grace of God."

"May I ask what happened?" she asked cautiously.

I gave her the quick version of Nate's story.

When I finished, she said, "I am glad to hear Nate is improving. After watching you guys, you seem to have a great family too."

"Thanks," I replied.

Next I asked her to tell me her story. She said, "I am from Indiana. My husband Patrick and I were visiting Northern Michigan when he fell and hit his head. He was airlifted to Butterworth on August 1. Since then, he has been in a medically induced coma to try to control swelling in his brain. The doctors told me a couple of days ago that it was time to think about taking him off life support."

The latest CT scan indicated that Patrick had suffered an extensive brain injury, and the doctors gave Danette little hope that Patrick could survive.

"Oh my," I gasped.

"I just can't do it," she confessed, as she shook her head and looked down to the ground.

Even though she had remained calm while sharing her story, my heart broke for her, and I tried desperately to think of some encouraging words. "Are you alone?" It was all I could muster.

"No," she answered. "My father is here with me." I was glad to hear that she was not alone. I could not imagine facing something like that by myself.

"I believe that Nate is alive today because so many people are praying for him," I told her, trying to find something encouraging.

"There are people praying for Patrick too," she said softly.

"Would you mind if we prayed together?" I questioned.

She nodded and said, "That would be nice."

So we bowed our heads and asked the Holy Spirit to come upon us. I asked for healing and peace for this family. I acknowledged how God's power could heal Patrick; however, when the words "Thy will be done" from the Lord's Prayer were recited, I asked for strength to accept God's will. Finally, I asked God to extend all of the graces that had been bestowed upon Nathan through so many people's prayers to Patrick as well. As we parted, Danette thanked me, and we promised to continue to pray for each other.

While thinking about Danette and Patrick's situation later that afternoon, I decided to take the Divine Mercy image that I had taped next to the Fatima medal on Nathan's bed to her. At first, I had some trouble finding her since I did not know her last name. I almost gave up the search after taking a couple of laps around the SICU patient floor. I finally found her standing in the hallway outside of Patrick's room.

As I approached her, I handed her the Divine Mercy prayer card. "I am Catholic," I told her. "I do not know what faith you are, but I wanted you to have this picture if you would accept it."

"Patrick is Catholic, but I am not," she said.

I briefly relayed the history behind the image. "There is a prayer, the Divine Mercy Chaplet, on the back of the card," I told her. "This is the prayer I turn to each time I need a miracle."

"I would be happy to take it," she replied.

The next day Danette and I crossed paths. She was excited to see me because she had news that she wanted to share with me. Since she chose to keep Patrick on life support, the doctors decided to reduce Patrick's medications again to see if there were any brain functions. "It seemed like he was trying to move his eyebrows!" she exclaimed.

"Wow! That is great news!" I replied.

"That was the most movement I have seen since he has been here," she explained.

"My whole family will be praying for you," I said joyfully. I was truly happy for her.

The following day I saw her in the waiting room again, and she explained how Patrick had moved his feet. What was even more amazing was when she sought me out on the third day. "Patrick is sitting up in bed!" she cried. His doctors were absolutely dumbfounded! I immediately felt goose bumps all over as she told me her good news and thanked me for the prayers.

Since then, we have become friends on Facebook. She has followed Nate's progress just as I have followed Patrick's. It was awesome to see the improvements from both of them. In our last correspondence, Danette informed me that Patrick had recovered enough to go back to work. This was just another testimony that displayed God's amazing love for us!

I tried to share these experiences on Facebook with the following post:

I just wanted to tell everyone who has been praying for Nate that so many people have been added to our prayer list. You need to know this because our family has been "praying it forward" . . . we have been extending your prayers to others who are in need of miracles. I have met so many people in this hospital that have found comfort knowing these prayers, from so many people, are coming their way. It has been remarkable how just a quick and simple gesture of prayer has had such an impact on so many. Our family has witnessed God's healing touch on other patients. I am sure your prayers have been part of a few other miracles besides Nathan's.

Danette replied with the following post:

Yes, my husband Patrick is one of those miracles! And your prayers mean so much.

Honestly, there were many people who we met and prayed with either in the SICU or Renucci House. These prayers usually involved terrible situations, but it was incredible how connected we all seemed to be. I kept thinking, *This is what God wants. This is how it is supposed to be . . . people, even strangers, holding each other up in the most difficult of times.* Joy, an unusual presence during such trying times, filled many hearts. People did not take anything for granted and rejoiced in and eagerly shared every small accomplishment with others.

I believed with all of my heart that the many, many people who kept Nate in their constant prayers were also affecting so many more. They were not even aware of it! I came to realize that prayer should never be taken lightly. It is truly a powerful instrument that can change any circumstance if it is in union with God's divine will.

CHAPTER 18

Off to DeVos

Those who fear the Lord prepare their hearts
and humble themselves before him.[1]

After the outside adventure on Sunday, it was determined that Nate was ready for the next step. So on Monday afternoon, the shift nurse announced, "Nate will be transferring out of the Surgical ICU to the general floor. Since he is under eighteen, he will be moved to the Helen DeVos Children's Hospital."

Nate and I were both surprised. I knew that this would eventually be the next step, but I did not realize it would be so soon. "Is he really ready for this?" I questioned, feeling very uncomfortable with the idea. I still felt that Nate responded best under Jess's care. Although his labs were all improving, he still needed blood at times; Jess would no longer be there to see us through those times once we moved.

The transfer came late in the day. It all happened so fast that we were not mentally prepared for it. Since the hospitals

1. Sirach 2:17 (NABRE)

165

were attached, a couple of aides came, packed up Nate's belongings, and wheeled him over to DeVos.

The blue room was bright and cheerful as we entered Nate's new residence. There was a bold-colored privacy curtain that added to the room's atmosphere. It was a room definitely geared toward little kids. Nate was not overjoyed by this fact. On an positive note, the windows were tall and offered a great view of the city.

Despite the view, the first night in the new hospital was such a change that Nate and I hardly slept. Since he was on the general floor, the nurses did not monitor him as closely. This made us even more uncomfortable. I tried to reassure Nate (and myself for that matter) that the stress was due to the new environment and new nurses, not his actual health issues. We both knew the doctors were confident Nate was ready for this move. Still, we found it difficult to relax.

After the first couple of days, Nate adapted and continued to improve. His voice was stronger but not quite enough to yell at his brothers yet. He sat up more, but best of all, he started to smile, and oh, how we had missed that smile!

Nate was finally speaking more clearly. He surprised me one morning with a raspy, "Mom, I think it is time I talked to a priest. I would like to receive the sacrament of reconciliation."

"That should be easy to arrange," I assured him, since I had been receiving communion almost daily.

That afternoon the priest from the Butterworth chapel came to visit. I stepped out to give them some privacy. After the priest left, I went back into Nate's room. Nate looked more relaxed. He said, "Thanks Mom. I feel better . . . like a huge weight has been lifted off of my shoulders."

I could not help but smile knowing that he was doing his part to build a closer relationship with God.

Unfortunately, Nate soon developed more abdominal pains, and on Tuesday, a CAT scan revealed another buildup of fluid. So he was whisked away to interventional radiology where the radiology doctors immediately inserted two drain tubes, one on each side. The tubes were connected to bulb-shaped suctions, which allowed the fluid to drain. It was a disgusting sight. The bulbs had to be dumped often at first. After a few days, the drainage slowed, but it was inconvenient to have the bulbs permanently attached since they got in the way when Nate tried to move. But, he dealt with the new development patiently and did not complain.

Nate's legs were a different story. As he began to be a little more active, it became evident that his legs had sustained a serious injury. They were numb from his knees down to his feet. Furthermore, Nate's feet were not working properly. This drastically affected his mobility. Since Nate's original X-rays and CT scans did not show any evidence of injury, the doctors decided that the bull ride had not caused this condition. At first, the doctors assumed his leg issues were caused by ICU neuropathy, a result of being immobile for so long in the SICU despite the special boots he wore to prevent it. The doctors assured us that this was somewhat common and often a temporary issue. Nevertheless, it became apparent that there was more to the story. Nathan was going to need some serious therapy.

As soon as he could handle it, Nate underwent speech, physical, and occupational evaluations for his condition. He had lost more than thirty pounds and, because he had been immobile for so long, he was extremely weak. It was such a struggle for him to sit up in bed, let alone walk. I could tell by the look on his face that he was wondering how he was going to handle his everyday tasks. Eating, dressing, showering, and other things we take for granted every day were all very difficult tasks for him.

Therapists worked with Nate twice a day. The goal was for him to increase his strength so that he could dress, eat, and perform other basic tasks unassisted so he could go home. It was not long, unfortunately, before it became clear that Nate would probably need more intense therapy before he could reach that goal.

Another development that occurred later that week was Nate's inability to retain sodium. His low sodium problems became even worse. Because of this, he was not allowed to have any water. He could only have Gatorade, Powerade, pop, and sometimes juice. The doctor also increased his sodium tablets. The doctors not only controlled his liquids, but his food intake as well. Nate was on every kid's dream diet. They prescribed him a high calorie, high fat, high sodium diet and ordered him to eat as much as he possibly could. During one of Dr. Robertson's quick visits, he told Nate to "put butter and mayo on everything."

Needless to say, we bought him all of the McDonald's food he could eat. For years I had told the kids, "Don't eat that food. It is not good for you!" The doctor shot that theory right out of the water.

While Nate used to be able to polish off more than one foot-long sub from Subway in five minutes, he could hardly eat more than two bites. It was evident that his stomach had shrunk. But that was not his only obstacle. Abdominal pressure from the fluid buildup and depression seemed to hinder his appetite as well.

By then, Tim was working most of the week, and Dani's college classes had started. The boys would rotate between keeping me company and staying at home where school and farm chores had to be done.

One day after her classes, Dani came to the hospital. It was late, and she wanted to stay with Nate. I had stepped out of the room for a moment, and when I came back, Dani was lying on the foot of the bed. She had convinced Nate to scoot his feet up so she could rest because she was very tired after such a long drive. I laughed! The next thing I knew, she stood up at the foot of the bed and put on Nate's leg compressions. Nate had to use them to prevent blood clots from forming while lying in bed. A very inquisitive Dani wrapped them around her own legs and turned on the machine. Her reaction was funny.

Excited, she said, "Ah! It feels like a massage. Move over bro," she told Nate as she walked over to the side of the bed once again. "Make more room for me so I can rest in bed while getting a leg massage."

I laughed at her silliness. It must have entertained Nathan as well because he obliged and scooted over. After getting comfortable, she told Nate, "You do not have it so bad. I do not want to hear you whine anymore. This is awesome." With Nate on the mend, he once again became a primary target for sibling sarcasm, which forced an occasional smile from his face. It was truly a welcome site!

One evening, my brother Bryan and his family came to visit. The next thing I knew, the room was filled with barnyard balloon animals made from nursing gloves. It was remarkable how creative bored teenagers could be with a few medical gloves and markers. Nate almost felt like he was home with the barrage of animals and animal noises that filled the room. My niece Brooke placed a glove on her head. Dani took a straw from Nate's cup, inserted it under the glove next to Brooke's forehead, and started blowing the glove up. Pretty soon the fingers of the glove stood up and made it look like Brooke had a rooster's comb on the top of her head. She started making rooster noises, causing quite a comical scene. Brooke tried her best to get Nate to smile, and it was not long before she succeeded and he started laughing.

"Stop making me laugh," he said trying to hold back a smile. "It makes my stomach hurt!" This, of course, made everyone laugh harder.

As the week progressed, Nate began to feel more and more excruciating leg pains. I always thought he had a high pain tolerance, and when he started asking for relief, I knew it had to be severe. He complained even after taking pain medication. "It is killing me!" he said. *Another bump in the road*, I thought, as I wondered what I could do to help. Rubbing his legs seemed to help. Sometimes, when I rubbed his legs and his feet, I remembered how I use to rub them when he was little. At that time, I thought for sure he would be an Olympic runner. I came to treasure those little memories even more.

On a more positive note, since Lori and Andy VanSlooten lived close by and Andy worked at the hospital, they visited frequently. Andy informed us one evening that Nate was famous. He explained that the Spectrum internal newsletter titled InSite featured Nate's story. (See "8 seconds, 97 units" on page 171.)

By then, Labor Day, the most anticipated weekend of the summer, was nearly upon us. For the past thirteen years, extended family, families-in-law, and close friends had gathered to camp at my mom and dad's property for an extended weekend of swimming, motorcycles, bonfires, cookouts, horseshoes, fireworks, and a huge pig roast. Under usual circumstances, this weekend was the official family assembly that signaled the end of another great summer. The kids always loved it and could not wait until the next yearly event.

While our circumstances were not typical, Tim and I decided that the tradition should still be carried on regardless of our situation. We planned on having the boys stay with my parents since we were not going to be present at the event. We also tried to make other arrangements for the activities we were usually responsible for.

When Tim and I approached my parents with our plan, my mother gave us some disheartening news. "Bryan, Jason, and Steven have decided to cancel the party due to the current circumstances," she said.

Tim said, "It is because of our situation that the weekend has to happen. We have a lot to celebrate. It is just too important to cancel."

8 SECONDS, 97 UNITS

Summer is a time of food, fun and fairs in Michigan. One fair is just kicking off in a small community not far from here. Children are getting ready to show their animals and the evening festivities are drawing crowds from all around. The rodeo is in town and people gathered to see if the riders can really last for eight seconds. At 6:00pm the fun begins. By 7:00pm, disaster strikes.

A young rider is thrown and trampled as he attempts to hang on for his eight seconds. The bull rears up and lands on the rider's stomach. He does not move. He is taken by ambulance to the closest facility – a small rural hospital and Spectrum Health Aero Med is called. Once Spectrum Health Aero Med arrives, it is decided he is too unstable to ride in the helicopter. He is taken to surgery by a surgeon who is one of our former residents here at Spectrum Health.

The scene is not good. They find 4 liters of blood inside his belly (think two 2 liters of pop) from the trauma he has experienced. The team works quickly to try to control the bleeding and get the patient stable enough to transfer to the trauma team in Grand Rapids. The patient is given the entire supply of available blood at the hospital. Two hours later, he is loaded onto the helicopter with the Aeromed team headed to Butterworth and the waiting trauma team.

Once he arrives at the Butterworth Emergency Department, the ED and trauma teams work quickly. They administer more blood products and get the patient to the OR within 11 minutes. The surgical team works furiously to save this young man's life. His liver is damaged; he continues to have internal bleeding and other injuries.

2 ½ hours later and 74 units of blood products later, he is brought to the interventional radiology department for another procedure.

The patient is finally stabilized and sent to the Surgical Intensive Care Unit in the Meijer Heart Center. Later that night, the care team notices the patient's condition is changing. Through questioning attitudes and escalation concerns, it is determined the patient is in trouble again. The surgical team performs another life-saving procedure; this time at the patient's bedside and whisks him yet again to the OR.

Fast forward two weeks later – this young man is laying in a hospital bed, healing, recovering and texting his friends.

This patient's life was saved by the dedicated teamwork amongst staff of the sending hospital, Spectrum Health Direct, Spectrum Health Aero Med, Butterworth Emergency Department, Pediatric and Adult Trauma Services, Anesthesia, Laboratory Blood Bank, both HDVCH and Butterworth OR teams, Interventional Radiology, and the Surgical ICU.

This is what a Level I Trauma Center is about. This is what Spectrum Health is about. When we work together as an expert team and use our safety behaviors as habits, anything is possible.

And if you didn't catch it in the title, this young man received at least 97 units of blood product during the first few hours following his injury. And, I found out later a total of 140 units were given to him.

Please donate if you are able.[2]

2. (Obetts 2014)

After some discussion and another vote, it was unanimous. The initial decision was overturned, and it was decided that the party would be moved to Cedar Springs, where Steve and Jason lived. Instead of being our usual five-day event, Labor Day would be a two-day campout with Jason and Kris hosting an impromptu cookout. We were all hopeful that Nate could make a brief appearance.

Plans were made, and the kids' anticipation grew once more. Since we could not ride motorcycles or swim, Jason and Steve concocted a homemade waterslide, which replaced the usual entertainment.

The doctors, as expected, did not agree with our plan for Nate's appearance. They strongly felt that he should not leave the hospital yet. But not much can stop this crazy family. The next thing I knew, on Saturday, August 30, just three weeks after the awful accident, the Cassiday and Davis families gathered together at the hospital for a mini celebration. Since Nate could not come to the party, the party would come to him.

The nursing staff overheard our plan and was kind enough to arrange for us and our extended family to use a small conference room just down the hall from Nate. They even provided a few slushies for the younger kids. What a terrific staff! We could not have asked for better nurses. This was just one example of how, on many occasions, they went above and beyond the call of duty during Nate's stay.

It was truly a joyous hour with jokes, laughter, and lots of smiles! My mom even had a pulled pork sandwich specially delivered, hoping to entice Nate's appetite since he was so thin. It was all quite a treat. Nate was cheerful yet exhausted when the hour was over.

Not long after the party, plans for Nathan to leave DeVos and go to a rehabilitation center were finally underway. Many doctors and nurses stopped by when they got wind of the good news. They had to see Nate's amazing progress for themselves and wish him well. This news was truly remarkable since the doctors had originally predicted Nate would be in the SICU for at least six weeks. Dr. Fromm, who had saved Nate's life in the SICU, was among those who stopped. Harry, a member of the Spectrum Health Aero Med crew, and several others from Butterworth also stopped by. All of the teams that had anything to do with Nate's recovery were, in my humble opinion, phenomenal! This was the best of the best! I knew it would be hard for anyone to compete with the outstanding care Nate had received the past twenty-four days at Butterworth and DeVos!

By then, Nate found the pain in legs almost unbearable. Although he was doing an incredible job with the hospital therapy, it was very difficult and painful for him to walk just to the bathroom, even with assistance. Most of the time, Nate would only make it to the chair next to the bathroom before he needed a break. Because of this, he became more depressed. He tried not to, but the reality of the situation weighed heavy on him.

Nate also developed nightmares, and he found it difficult to be alone for long periods of time. I wondered if this was a side effect from the pain medication for his legs.

Dr. Robertson came to check on him the next day. After examining the drains and Nate's abdomen, he asked him how he was feeling mentally and emotionally. "Just fine," Nate answered indifferently.

But Dr. Robertson knew better. After talking with him and asking Nate more questions, Dr. Robertson declared, "Nate, you're going to Mary Free Bed!"

I had never heard of the place, but the nurses explained that it was a world-renowned rehabilitation center located a few blocks away. They all agreed that that was the best place for Nate to be.

A rehab specialist from Mary Free Bed stopped in the following day to evaluate him. "Hello, I am Dr. Ayla," she said as she introduced herself. "I will be caring for Nate when he transfers to Mary Free Bed."

She then asked Nate some questions while she evaluated him. As she began to check his feet, she said, "I am now going to poke you with a pin in a few places. Can you look away and let me know when you can feel a slight poke?"

She started at his toes, no response. She moved to his ankles, again, no response. She then moved up to his knees when Nate finally said, "I can feel pressure but not really a poke."

She determined that Nate still had feeling above the knees but not much below. She said, "After examining you, I do not believe you have ICU neuropathy."

"What is it then?" I asked.

"I believe he has nerve damage due to the abdominal compartmental syndrome. Do you see how both feet and legs experienced the same degree of injury? Most likely, when his abdomen swelled, it pinched the nerves in his back so severely that they were damaged. That is why he has the same symptoms in both legs. The good news is that the nerves were not severed; the bad news is that this type of injury heals very, very slowly. I will have a plan ready for him when he arrives in a couple of days." After saying our goodbyes, she left.

And then another bump came along. A day before Nate was to be transferred, our insurance decided that he could recover at home with some outpatient therapy. Boy, were we nervous. Nate was still facing many medical issues like low sodium, fevers, and low hemoglobin. Dr. Robertson found out about our situation and knew Mary Free Bed was an important next step to Nate's mental as well as physical recovery. When he stopped in to check on Nate, Dr. Robertson seemed irritated with the situation. He stated very confidently, "I will take care of this! You are going to Mary Free Bed, and that is it!"

Dr. Robertson was very concerned with treating the whole patient, not just Nate's liver. I was very appreciative of his protectiveness, as it reduced my concerns knowing that Nate had an advocate whenever problems surfaced.

The day finally came for Nate to leave the security of the hospital. It was discharge day. It was hard to think about adjusting to new surroundings again. Yet we knew it was one more step to getting home. When we were all packed and ready to leave, Mallory, Nate's nurse, helped him into the wheelchair.

Before a technician who was following Mallory pushed Nate out of his room, Mallory paused at the counter and loaded nine completely full inch-and-a-half yellow envelopes onto the discharge cart. I had to deliver them to Mary Free Bed.

As she placed the heavy folders onto the top of the cart that held some of Nate's belongings, she exclaimed, "Whew! I have never seen anyone with that much medical history. Usually a patient only has one . . . not that many!"

We joyfully joked about it as we headed toward the door, yet in the back of our minds, as we proceeded through the hospital, we were well aware of how many miracles it took to get Nate to this day. Unfortunately, I never thought to take a picture of the huge stack of papers; it was truly impressive.

Since Tim could not get the day off work, my mom drove down to Grand Rapids to help. Mom had already pulled her car up to the main entrance. As we said our goodbyes to Mallory, we loaded all of our belongings. Nate carefully climbed into the passenger's seat, and we were off for the next leg of this incredible journey.

CHAPTER 19

Mary Free Bed

Let us fall into the hands of the Lord
and not into the hands of mortals.[1]

On Wednesday, September 3, almost four weeks after that fateful day, Nate became an inpatient at Mary Free Bed Hospital for some intense rehabilitation. With this move, we allowed ourselves to think week by week instead of just day by day. My mom and I helped Nate move into his new residence, and the first thing I did was tape the Fatima medal to the head of Nate's bed just as it had been during his stay at Butterworth and DeVos.

While we were unpacking, the mood became somewhat somber. Nervousness became a way of life each time we encountered change. In spite of the fact that he was getting better, Nate still faced a few serious challenges. His sodium levels were still dangerously low, his fevers continued to spike, and his hemoglobin count was low. What if his electrolytes went crazy? What if his fever went too high again? What

1. Sirach 2:18 (NABRE)

if he needed more blood? Could this facility handle such emergencies since they were not a trauma unit? These were some of the questions that troubled us. Yet we had to continue to hope in God by trusting the doctors' decisions and push forward.

During one of his last visits with Nate at DeVos, Dr. Robertson had warned Nate about challenges he might face when he went home. "Nate, it is scary to think about life outside of the hospital, but now it is time to do so," he said. "You need to learn how to trust your body again. This is a common psychological fear when one encounters such a traumatic event. Being able to trust your own body is such a natural phenomenon that it is taken for granted until something devastating happens."

He assured us that Nate was physically ready for this and that it was an important step for him to continue to heal physically, mentally, and emotionally. So here we were, apprehensive but moving forward!

The pain in Nate's legs and feet was still intense. Dr. Ayla, the rehabilitation doctor who initially evaluated him in DeVos, would be his primary doctor at this facility. She had informed Nate during her initial evaluation that the pain he was experiencing would most likely become worse before it improved due to the many different types of nerves that had been damaged. This was not something he really wanted to hear. Despite medication, he still found the pain excruciating.

She explained that this type of healing tended to be a very long process. "Only a millimeter a day . . . that is how long it will take to heal these nerves. Look how long your leg is. It is going to take some time. You are fortunate since the nerves were only compressed and not severed. I am very hopeful that you will regain ninety-nine percent of the movement in your feet. But this will require patience, determination, and hard work," she encouraged him.

"The medication does not seem to be working," he told Dr. Ayla.

"It eventually will after the doses have been properly adjusted," she reassured him before she left.

The staff took it easy on their new patient the first day. The next morning, however, was a different story. Breakfast was served promptly at 7:30 a.m. Following breakfast, Nate was expected to shower and be ready for his physical therapy session at 8:30 a.m. A nurse helped him since he could hardly stand on his own, let alone walk. His morning routine would also include occupational, recreational, and psychological therapies. After that he would have an extended lunch break so that he could rest before his repeated afternoon therapies. The evenings in his new surroundings would be fairly quiet. After dinner, Nate would not be interrupted except to distribute medications and check his vitals. It was important for him to rest after a hard day.

Almost everything Nate did before the accident, he had to relearn. This was due to his weakened condition and physical limitations. Those muscles just did not want to do what Nate wanted them to without him having to think about it! For me, watching Nate struggle was tough. Yet, after meeting some of the other patients, I realized that no matter what Nate's struggles were, sadly, there would always be someone who's condition was much worse.

By the third day, overwhelmed between the physical work and the excruciating pain, Nate experienced a meltdown. Feeling defeated, he moaned, "I can't! I just can't do this. It is too much! I just want to sleep." Needless to say, the therapy team gave into Nate's mood and he skipped therapy that morning. There was no skipping the afternoon sessions though. The therapists would not take no for an answer. They were very persuasive and eventually convinced him to push forward.

With that difficult morning behind him, Nate eventually

found some comfort in his daily routines, except for the Gatorade diet. By then, he was sick of the drink he once loved. He craved water, particularly after exercising. But like the pain in his legs, this would just have to be something he had to suffer through.

A constant schedule provided another advantage. It allowed Nate to become aware of other people around him. Because it was a rehabilitation center, every person had his or her own difficult circumstance. Many of them were much more challenging than Nate's. This realization helped Nathan push through the rest of his trials more patiently, especially the debilitating shooting foot pains.

One of the people who we met had a much more challenging time. His name was Max LaMee. Max was from Coleman, a little town just south of ours. He was a few years older than Nate. He had been attending Michigan State University and had been very active in the MSU rodeo program, especially as a bull rider, before his accident.

Memorial Day weekend was a big celebration in my parents' hometown of Gladwin. Every year there was a large gathering for the local Super Kicker Rodeo. It was a two-night event on Friday and Saturday. This particular Memorial Day weekend, May 2014, would turn tragic as Max rode on a bucking bronco. During the event, Max had sustained a severe blow to his back that paralyzed him.

Our paths crossed four months later. When I met Max, he was sitting in his room after dinner with his mom, Jeanne. I noticed right away that he had some use of his wrists, but Jeanne explained that he only had feeling from the chest up. Upon meeting him, all I could think about was how impressed I was. He had a terrific smile and a joking manner about him in spite of his circumstances. He had an incredible outlook on life, and I sensed that his circumstances would not get the best of him.

Jeanne proved to be just as wonderful as her son. She took the time to show me around one day while the boys had therapy. Mary Free Bed was attached to St. Mary's hospital, which had a cancer wing called the Mercy Health Lacks Cancer Center. Located at the top floor of this center was a special room. It was similar to a terrarium with huge plants all over the place. Jeanne told me that the hospital created it to help the cancer patients experience the outdoors while they were stuck in the hospital. It was pretty impressive as it had great big windows so all of the massive plants could get some sunlight. They also had an inspirational hallway with pictures and plaques on the walls. One group of pictures displayed The Stations of the Cross, which allowed a person to reflect on the passion of Christ. Others were quotes and pictures of heroic people like Mother Teresa. I could see the value of this new center as being a beautiful source of encouragement for anyone facing a major trial.

Jeanne also directed me to the chapel. I would frequent this room often during Nate's stay at Mary Free Bed. Mass was offered at noon almost daily. This schedule worked out nicely for me since Nate was usually in therapy then. Mass was televised for the patients at St. Mary's, so the priest's message revolved around the ill. Whenever this was brought up during Mass, I would think about how I use to take praying for the sick for granted. I would not do so again. This hour became a very peaceful time of the day for me and gave me the grace to maintain a positive attitude for Nate.

Both Jeanne and Max became a source of determination for Nate and me. I was also grateful to Jeanne for her kindness because she took the time to show me around; otherwise, I probably would not have come across such peaceful places.

Another patient we met was a little boy around five or six years old. He had been involved in a very serious accident and was lucky to be alive. He was one tough kid! I was not sure about the extent of his injuries, but when I met him, he was learning how to walk again with assistance from braces and canes. He was truly an inspiration for many people, as they would stop whatever they were doing and watch him walk ever so slowly down the hallway with such determination. Although he must have been in a lot of pain, he often smiled and high fived the staff as he continuously pushed himself to improve. He was a little ray of sunshine and could change even the crankiest of moods as he passed by.

There were many others that I met. What I found remarkable was how determined and full of hope they were even through their hardships.

Dr. Ayla came in to check on Nate's progress almost every day. It did not take long for her to become fond of him too, and, like Dr. Robertson, she would make sure any health problems Nate encountered were resolved whether they fell under her umbrella of responsibilities or not, even after we left Mary Free Bed.

Because of his injury, Nate could not walk well. He had to lift each knee and let his feet flop out in front of him to take a step. One of Dr. Ayla's first recommendations was leg braces to help support his feet until he regained his strength. Such a thought was humbling for a seventeen-year old's ego. To make things more interesting, Dr. Ayla insisted that Nate continue to use them well past the time he felt he no longer needed them. I laughed one day at Nate's frustration over this situation. I reminded him how blessed he was to have so many people looking out for him! Exasperated he said, "I know. I know! But I don't need these silly braces." He could be a little stubborn!

During the first week at Mary Free Bed, Nate continued to struggle with his sleep. At first the staff monitored him closely, waking him up every few hours to check his blood pressure, draw blood, or give him medication. After a few days, his hemoglobin labs and temperature improved so the nurses did not need to wake him as much. Yet the relentless leg and foot pain continued to cause him grief, especially at night. All of this probably contributed to the nightmares Nate continued to have. Many nights I slept on a cot in his room so he did not have to be alone. I grew to appreciate this time since we would pray or have heart-to-heart conversations. We even watched most of the Psych TV series, which provided some much-needed comic relief. His laughter brought tears of joy to my eyes. Thus, the restless nights became precious moments for me.

After a week of therapy, Nate began to see the fruits of his labors. He was getting stronger. He could walk a short distance down the hallway, with help of course. He slowly started pushing himself through the pain so he could reach his goal: home!

The wheelchair was always close by since the sharp, intermittent shooting pains in his feet were still more than he could endure. When this type of pain struck, it would almost buckle his legs under him. Dr. Ayla assured him that the more he walked, the more his body would adjust to the pain and it would eventually subside.

His weight was another constant battle. Since his stomach had shrunk and his physical activity had increased, Nate continued to shed the pounds. It was hard to imagine him losing any more weight since he was already so thin. Right away, it became a major concern. The attending nurse told Nate, "It is important that you eat all of your meals. You are still losing weight. If you continue to lose weight, you will have to be placed back on a feeding tube."

"I know. I know. The problem is that the food does not even sound good," Nate argued.

No one wanted to think about a feeding tube. Up until then, I thought eating was an Olympic sport for all seventeen-year-old boys, and Nate could have easily qualified as a semifinalist before the accident.

One morning after Nate had been working so hard, the recreational therapist announced, "It is time for Nate to go off campus. We will take a walk for lunch." The therapist continued, "Maybe that will entice your appetite."

A few hours later, I tagged along as Nate and the wheelchair were whisked away to Subway, his favorite fast-food restaurant. It was only a few blocks away. Regardless of the fact that he could only eat a couple of bites, it was great to see him outside, in the sun, enjoying the day.

On the way back to the hospital, the therapist asked, "Do you think you could walk a little?"

"Sure," Nate said cheerfully as he pushed himself up and stepped away from the wheelchair. He was a little unsteady at first, but then found a good walking pace. I held my breath as he approached the uneven sidewalks. We were all pleasantly surprised when he kept his balance and continued walking.

"You are doing a great job!" the therapist complemented, as he walked passed the targeted goal. Nate met not only his goal but also much more. It was a huge accomplishment, and it meant Nate was one step closer to going home.

With his determined spirit, Nate's progress greatly improved over the next couple of days. Finally, pleased with his physical progress, Dr. Ayla decided Nate would be discharged on Friday. "Perhaps some home cooking would put some meat on his bones," she suggested. Since by then he could eat, dress, and move around better, she was sure that sleeping in his own bed would be the best therapy. The move would also allow him to continue to heal mentally and emotionally; this was going to take some time.

After Dr. Ayla's decision, I made arrangements for Nate to have outpatient therapy twice a week at Mary Free Bed. Since he had become a little more mobile, he needed to focus on increasing his balance and improving his walking abilities. The therapy days would be scheduled back to back; that way Nate and I would drive to Grand Rapids on a Monday, spend the night at one of my brothers' houses, and go back to therapy on Tuesday. We would return home late that afternoon. This plan permitted Nate to have three days of uninterrupted school at home, which Nate needed because he was very determined to graduate the following May.

The day before Nate was scheduled to go home, I attended Mass in the chapel while he was at therapy. It was then that I had heard that members of the TV show *Tanked* had been in the Mercy Health Lacks Cancer Center lobby working on a secret project. Afterward, I lingered at the balcony outside of the chapel that overlooked the main floor lobby area to watch the *Tanked* team work. The team was just about finished with their project. They had designed a fish tank specifically for the center. It was huge! It had a Grand Rapids City theme to it and was very impressive.

I hurried back to tell Nate when he finished his therapy for the day. "Shall we take a stroll to see the *Tanked* team?" I asked.

"Sure," he said, tired, but willingly.

Nate moved to his wheelchair, and away we went through Mary Free Bed into the attached St. Mary's hospital to the Lacks Cancer Center lobby hoping to catch the *Tanked* team's final assembly stages.

Once at the lobby, we found a quiet corner and watched the guys work. After a while, one of the workers came over and shook Nate's hand. They talked for a few minutes. He asked if we watched the show, and Nate told him we did. The gentleman then asked Nate if he would like to meet the hosts, Wayde King and Brett Raymer. "Sure," Nate said with a smile.

After a few minutes, he led us to a small conference room. The worker knocked on the door and told us to wait outside as he disappeared into the room. When the door opened again, two jocular guys dressed in black shirts entered the hallway.

Wayde and Brett were welcoming with their big smiles and enthusiastic handshakes. Their joking and small talk put a candid smile on Nate's face. It was good to see, and I greatly appreciated the efforts by the *Tanked* team. After talking for a few minutes, they informed us that they were in the middle of filming a show and had to get back to work. We thanked them for their time after they posed for a few pictures. With one final handshake, they disappeared behind the wooden door again.

As I pushed Nate back toward his room at Mary Free Bed for one last night, I once again reflected on how it truly was the simple, little things that we do for each other that can brighten a person's day and give them little glimpses of hope.

CHAPTER 20

Finally Home

For equal to his majesty is his mercy;
and equal to his name are his works.[1]

The whole family came to help pack Nate up and bring him home. Once we left Mary Free Bed, we had quite a few pharmacy stops to make in order to locate all of the medications that Nate needed. We were all anxious to get home.

When we finally pulled into the driveway, many people had already gathered to warmly welcome Nate home. The first thing he did when he stepped out of the Ford was pet our dog, Lexy. She seemed to understand what was happening and waited next to the parked vehicle for Nathan to open the door. As soon as Nate bent over to greet the German shepherd, her face lit up and her brown tail wagged as if to say, "I missed you; welcome home!"

He slowly made his way up our front porch steps and walked gingerly toward the front door where a long line of

1. Sirach 2:19 (NABRE)

people waited to greet him. With a heartwarming smile and a face beaming with gratitude, he stopped and hugged each and every person.

The rest of the afternoon was spent greeting a trickle of friends, family, and neighbors who popped in to say hi. By the end of the day, Nate was exhausted. He was more than ready to settle down in his own bed.

The next day, as Nate continued to adjust to being at home, we realized that the Fatima medal was not among any of the items we had brought with us from Mary Free Bed. After thinking about it, I realized that, in all of the commotion surrounding the move, I never removed it from his bed. I was sad for forgetting it. Tim looked up the nurse's contact number that the staff had given to us in our farewell package. When he called, the nurse confirmed that we had indeed left it. She explained that a staff member had found it and meant to call us to let us know where it was since everyone knew how special it was to us. She offered to put it in the mail before it became lost in the shuffle.

We waited and waited for the medal to arrive. A week went by with no sign of it. When I called to ask about it, the receptionist told me that they could not find it. This was disheartening information, of course, as it had become a token of divine grace for our family. I resigned myself to the fact that Mary had interceded when we needed her the most, so if this was how it was meant to be, so be it.

To our surprise, about a month later, the Fatima medal appeared one day in the mail! We were thankful, and Nate has faithfully worn it around his neck ever since.

On September 14, not long after his move home, Stacey Demoines from the Clare County 4-H and my sister-in-law Kelli organized a benefit to help cover the hospital expenses. Again, the generosity we received overwhelmed our family. People donated great food, great prizes for a silent auction, and even great music.

When Nate stepped out of the Ford on the crisp fall day and burrowed into the blankets in his wheelchair, the David Yonker Band broke out into song to celebrate his arrival. Jeff Bates was the bass guitarist; he had been with us during the first two days of our ordeal. It was quite a sight to see so many people come out to support us. Instead of a benefit, it felt like a celebration as people gathered around to shake Nate's hand.

The first person to step forward for the handshaking honors was Brad Doepker, our favorite paramedic. For Brad, a handshake would not suffice. So Brad bent down and gave Nate a big bear hug and said, "It sure is good to see ya!"

"Thanks . . . for everything," Nate said. There was not a dry eye in the place with such a touching scene.

Even State Representative Joel Johnson took the time to come to greet Nate. Rep. Johnson actually had been at Nate's Eagle Scout Court of Honor just a week prior to the accident. He had presented Nate with a state certificate that recognized his achievements in obtaining Eagle Scout, which is the highest rank in Boy Scouts. Only ten percent of scouts achieve this rank.

As Nate made his way through the crowd, Rep. Johnson came forward and said, "It is great to see you Nate! It was only a few months ago I shook your hand for your Eagle Award. Who could have known then what a change in circumstances you have endured. I am so happy to be able to shake your hand on this very fine day!"

"It is good to see you, too. Thanks! Thanks for all your support!" Nate replied graciously.

As the afternoon went on, Nate had a chance to publicly thank everyone. Our local 9&10 News team came and interviewed him at the benefit. He attributed his presence and progress to God and all of the prayers so many people had offered throughout his ordeal.

Slowly, we began to find a rhythm in life again. Nate and I

would trek down to Grand Rapids overnight once a week for doctor appointments and therapy, and he eventually started his studies so he could finish his senior year on time. Tim was not only back to work but also busy taking care of our hobby farm. Dani continued her nursing classes, and Nick, Mathew, and Andrew were able to finally focus on school, scouts, hunting, and wrestling.

Life was good again! Although we would still face many trials at times, we were all very aware of how blessed our family truly was. Those blessings came to us through the actions, prayers, and support of many people. We could not have made it through such an ordeal without them. It was only then that we learned how to completely trust in Divine Providence, in ways we could not ever have imagined. In turn, God provided all that we needed and more. One of the most profound blessings of all was finding hope on a bull named Vegas.

AFTERWORD

Unintended Consequences

IMPACT ON NATHAN

After the accident, two ideas Nathan cherished most, freedom and independence, were gone. To say he was humbled was an understatement. He needed help with even the simplest of tasks. As noted earlier, depression visited him often. Thankfully, it did not take up a permanent residence. He was determined to be productive once again. As expected, Nate's experience provided him with a new outlook on life on many levels: physically, mentally, and spiritually.

Physically, Nate could not drive, walk very far, or do most things he wanted. He was no longer able to visit friends on a whim or attend social events he once enjoyed. He realized how hard he would have to physically push himself, especially through the relentless nerve pain, in order to get back to a normal life once more.

Slowly, Nate was able to live more normally. He continued a rigorous workout routine even after completing his last physical therapy session. As soon as he could handle it, someone took him to the local gym several days during the week. He began to find some pride in seeing results from his exercise routines. While he could not run because of his feet, he did start a cardio routine on an elliptical machine, which strengthened his leg muscles. Nate was hopeful that he would be completely healed physically, and I am proud to report that he is almost there. He has not signed up for any marathons yet, but who knows what the future holds. He is determined to be as active and physically fit as he can.

Initially, Nate believed he would die, especially after he left DeVos Children's Hospital. Once he came home from Mary Free Bed, he still felt that way at times; he wondered if he only had a year or two to live. He needed a purpose to keep such thoughts at bay. He found one in school, something that he never dreamed would motivate him!

Mentally, school became Nathan's number one priority. This was a new experience for all of us! Before the accident, Nate was not one to enjoy academics, and school seemed to get in his way. Work gave Nate purpose then and he was good at it. One of his jobs was to look after the newborn calves at a local dairy farm, and he enjoyed it at the time. With such distractions, it took quite a bit of effort to get him to focus and complete his schooling in a timely manner. After the accident, all this changed. School became the only productive activity that he could do. So, since his social life and work took a serious standstill, he shifted all of his attention to completing his studies to graduate on time!

Graduation day was a tearful event for all of us. Each year the Christian Home Educators of Midland homeschool group holds a personalized graduation ceremony for the seniors. Between ten and twenty graduates typically participated in the annual event. Every graduate's family was allowed to prepare a two-minute video that pertained to the graduate's life. Dani and I prepared Nate's video. Part of country singer Tim McGraw's song "Live Like You Were Dying" played in the background while pictures scrolled across the screen displaying Nate's life from his early childhood to his cowboy days. It was a very emotional two minutes for me as I watched the video play on the huge screen at the graduation ceremony. After the video, Tim and I walked across the stage where Nate met us in the middle. As we handed him his diploma before a crowded room, I was confident that we were perhaps the happiest parents in the room. Tim flipped Nate's tassel and gave him a huge hug. Nate handed me a flower and thanked us for everything. He graduated! Our whole family felt blessed to be able to share in that precious moment. We were keenly aware of how close we came to losing it!

School was not the only thing he appreciated a little more; family, community, and life all took on a new meaning. Family became first in his life again. It became his center. No longer would he be too busy to hang out with his brothers or cousins. Family dinners and extended family gatherings became a high priority. So did his sense of community. Throughout Nate's ordeal, he felt overwhelmed by how many people continued to reach out to us with good wishes, even after he arrived home. Every time Nate went to church or the store, people would take a moment to talk to him to check on his progress and offer some encouraging words. Nate was always gracious.

One of his most profound experiences from the accident, however, was spiritual. Not only did his faith in God grow, but also his faith in people. Nate realized that we were surrounded by good people: friends, neighbors, and communities. He surmised that most people, especially in our small community, have big hearts. Everyone matters and random acts of kindness play a crucial role in other people's lives. These were deep thoughts for a teenager. Nate realized that on no occasion should our lives or people be taken for granted. Both were truly a gift from God and needed to be appreciated.

Almost a year and a half after the accident, the Right to

Life of Midland County organization asked Nathan to give a short synopsis of his ordeal for their annual Focus on Life dinner. As he presented his story to a captivated crowd, he explained how he used to think miracles only happened in history, not in today's world. This was no longer true!

"Miracles do happen . . . now . . . today . . . and we need to be aware of that fact," Nate stressed to the crowd.

During his speech, he recognized the powerful tool that all of us have: prayer! Nate emphasized that his life was spared because so many people prayed.

Many times I have heard Nate say, "I cannot believe what God has done for me. I do not deserve it."

Nathan gained not only a second chance in life but also the opportunity to become a better person. With a new appreciation for life, Nate grew in patience, understanding, and compassion for others.

IMPACT ON OTHERS

Once doctors discharged him from Mary Free Bed, Nate tried to continue with life as he normally would have. Each fall, our family attended duck camp. Tim had been taking the kids to duck camp ever since Dani was ten years old. This was a cherished annual event. Many fellow duck hunters camped together for several weeks. Since we knew a close friend of ours who was a very seasoned nurse would be there, we packed up and went for an extended weekend.

The weekend not only provided us with a duck hunting opportunity but also a chance to meet up with Father Christian Tabares. We knew Father Christian when he served at the church in Clare a few years earlier. He followed our story and prayed for Nate often. He was currently assigned to the Our Lady Consolata in Sebewaing, Michigan, which was a short drive from duck camp. I had hoped Father Christian would be there but was not sure since I had not contacted him once he moved. The rest of the family did not have a clue, and I was hoping to surprise them all.

It was a small church. Father was unaware as we quietly slid into our pews that Sunday. When he walked in and turned to face the congregation, he noticed Nate right away. He was visibly taken aback. He was silent for a moment as he looked to the ground. Then, with a proud grin that beamed from his face, he looked at the congregation and stated, "My friends, I just want you to know that if you do not believe in miracles, I present one to you today." He extended a hand in Nathan's direction as he briefly explained how Nate should not have, but did, cheat death through God's mercy and an abundance of prayer.

After Mass, we talked with Father Christian as he asked for some of the details concerning the accident. He could not wipe the smile off of his face. It was such an honor to see Father Christian, especially since he offered many prayers in our name.

After duck camp, Nate and I continued our adventures to Grand Rapids for therapy and doctor appointments. One afternoon, Nate had an appointment to have an ultrasound of his kidneys at DeVos Children's Hospital. While we were there, as chance would have it, we ran into Pastor John Devries while exiting the elevator. At first, he did not recognize me, but when he did, his face beamed with delight. He explained how stunned he was to see Nathan, alive! As we talked, he told us that when Nate was airlifted to Butterworth, the hospital staff asked him if he could meet with us. They told him to be prepared to comfort a grieving family since no one expected Nate to live through the night. With that in mind, he said he "was more than tickled to be able to shake Nate's hand!"

After we said our joyful goodbyes and turned to leave, Pastor John turned back and stated, "They should make a movie out of this, or at least a book."

All of us laughed at what we thought was a crazy idea.

During the last week of January, on our way back from another therapy trip to Grand Rapids, we decided to take an impromptu route through Alma. It was the first time we had been back to the area since Nate's accident nearly six months prior. I was not sure how either Nate or I would handle it. Since it was a long drive, I had plenty of time to call ahead to check if Dr. Bonacci and the trauma unit had time for a visit. Both eagerly said yes to our request.

Our first stop was Dr. Bonacci's office. He was the surgeon who operated on Nate to try to stop his internal bleeding. Upon shaking Nate's hand, Dr. Bonacci was amazed to see Nate standing on his own two feet. While we visited for a few minutes, Dr. Bonacci commented on how he had trained with Dr. Rodriguez and Dr. Robertson. I told him that Dr. Rodriguez mentioned how crucial that fact was for it could have been the difference between life and death. I described the confidence Dr. Rodriguez displayed, knowing who had first assessed Nate and how the decisions were made that night.

Next, I asked Dr. Bonacci about his thoughts the night of the accident. He smiled and said, "It was nice to be able to go home and tell my family that I helped save a kid's life." Months later, Dr. Bonacci would tell me, "I would absolutely agree, without reservation, that it [Nathan's recovery] was indeed a miracle."

After our visit with Dr. Bonacci, we stopped by Gratiot Medical Center. The staff was very accommodating and was more than excited to have us visit. They treated us with so much hospitality. Although they only had a short time to prepare for our arrival, arrangements had been made for us to tour the facility and visit various people including the administration and ER staff, many of whom helped save Nate's life that fateful night.

When we entered the ER wing, the staff introduced us to Dr. Metwally, the doctor who was on duty the night of the accident. Without any word or warning, he boldly walked right up to Nate, lifted his shirt, and said, "We would like to see!" as he examined Nate's impressive scar. The staff was extremely excited to finally meet Nathan. It was truly a rewarding experience for all of us.

During one of the many trips to Grand Rapids, we were able to meet up with Father Donald E. Lomasiewicz from Saint Isidore Parish. I must admit, I thought Father Don would be a little surprised to see Nate, but he was not. He was very certain in the power of prayer! I told him how grateful I was that he took the time to administer last rites during those frightful late-night hours. Without hesitation, he simply smiled and stated that it was his job.

February brought a new month of appointments; our favorite was a trip to Dr. Robertson's office after Nate finally had his drain tubes removed. He was so happy to be rid of those things!

Nate was doing very well by then and had made a lot of progress physically. Although he was still thin, he had gained back some weight. He simply looked healthier, and his smile and sense of humor proved it. Dr. Robertson's staff was surprised and commented on how good he looked as Nathan, Dani, Andrew, and I made our way back to the patient rooms smiling all the way.

Dr. Robertson, of course, was always happy to see Nate and could not have been more proud as he entered the room. We discussed how well Nate was mending compared to where he was at his last visit. We then discussed what to expect over the next few months.

During our discussion, as he shook his head in amazement, Dr. Robertson commented, "I do not know why some make it and others, who are not as bad off, do not."

Almost a year after the accident, at Nate's final visit with Dr. Robertson, I mustered up enough courage to ask the question that constantly plagued me since that fateful Saturday night.

As the appointment wrapped up and Dr. Robertson asked if we had any questions, I simply asked, "That first night of the accident, when you came down to meet Tim and me and explained to us what happened to Nate, what percentage did you give Nate . . . to make it?"

Dr. Robertson looked at me and plainly said, "I gave him less than a five percent chance to make it through the night!"

I knew I would have a hard time processing the answer! All I could say was "Wow!" as tears filled my eyes.

After we said our goodbyes to the staff at the doctor's office, we finished the day by stopping by the SICU one last time. Although we had been back a few times since the accident and talked to some of the nurses, not once were we able to find our super nurse, Jess. We were pleasantly surprised to find her on duty that day.

While walking down the hallway toward the room Nate had occupied, we spied Jess walking the floor. At first, she did not recognize us as we approached her, but, when she did, she stumbled back in disbelief. Tears filled her eyes.

We had spent so much time with Jess while Nate was hospitalized that my whole family loved her. She was so determined that Nate was going to make it. If she ever doubted it, she certainly did not show it! Whenever Nate's vitals would start to decline, Jess instinctively knew what to do to improve them. She was an angel to us. Our family will be forever indebted to her and the terrific staff at Butterworth Hospital!

Our final trip to Grand Rapids was for a nephrology appointment in November of 2015. It provided us with an excuse to visit the flight crew. I tried to bring myself to arrange this reunion earlier, but for some reason, I could not. I kept telling myself, "Next time . . ." This time I followed through.

The crew was pleased to see us. They gave us a warm welcome and a tour of the facility. They briefly walked us through the events that occurred the night of the accident, answered questions, and even let the kids crawl into one of the helicopters. According to Andrew, he enjoyed the visit the most since he was allowed to sit in the pilot's seat and learn all about the GPS. When he crawled out of the helicopter, Andrew proudly announced that he wanted to be a pilot someday. Everyone chuckled.

As we continued our visit, Meghan relayed her personal thoughts concerning that night. She said she was so joyful to see Nate because she really did not think he was going to make it. She said that the fact that he was bleeding through the abdomen packing before they were even on the helicopter was just not a good sign. She also commented on how Nate's vital signs did not deteriorate as she expected during the flight. But he made it, and here he was smiling with the crew.

We also discussed how painful it was when Meghan had to tell me that I could not ride with Nate that night. She confessed that had there been more time, it could have happened. Since time was of the essence, they could not explain safety precautions and, therefore, I could not go.

With our visit wrapping up, the crew led us back to the lobby area where they presented us with a few gifts such as hats, pencils, and other trinkets to remember them by. Like we could ever forget!

One comment that struck me was when the crew thanked us for visiting. Meghan explained how many times they do not get closure with their patients. She continued to say how nice it was to see that the choices they made the night of the accident were the right ones.

As the last note to the book, I have enclosed some personal reflections by people who reached out to us. Nate's accident had an unexpected impact. I have been told by many people, through Facebook and in person, that our experience has greatly strengthened their relationship with God. Many who reached out were complete strangers, which I find incredible. As Nick pointed out one evening, "How could one homeschooled kid make such a difference?"

So in closing, I wish to thank you, the reader, for your interest in our story, and leave you with the following sentiments that people shared with us throughout our miraculous journey:

> Michelle Davis, Tim, and children my heart aches for you. It has been some time since I have prayed . . . You all hold such fond, loving memories in my heart that I am finding that light that I have shut out. I am praying for Nathan and you! I love you guys!
>
> —Kari Seymour-Schloff

> Will continue to pray for the ENTIRE family as well as Nate. You all need strength and direction going through this, realizing it is out of your hands. This is deepening faith in God for us all. Godspeed.
>
> —Bill Sommerfeldt

> This is THE most wonderful thing that I have heard all week! What a relief! Nathan is definitely a Miracle! The Love and Faith of family and friends has encouraged all of us! My HERO!
>
> —Audrey Fraley

> Thanks for the updates. I realize with him getting better there are less frequent updates and that is a GREAT thing. . . . I wish I could express how much your updates and Nate's progress impact me emotionally and continually strengthen my faith but there really are no words that would do it justice. Love you all . . . God bless you all . . . now and for always. He is truly amazing.
>
> —Vicki Donovan

We are strangers we've not met. But through prayer, we are friends and family through God. Every day I look for the updates and pray it is good news. It is wonderful that every day we are given a new day[.] Can you imagine every day is new and you[r] son is given new hope along with you his parents and family friends and strangers like me[?] We have an awesome God and Nate is part of this awesomeness.

—JudyAnn Raymond

I pray for him and your family often throughout the day. He is never far from my thoughts even though I have not met him. Our God is an awesome God! To Him be the glory!

—Jody

He has been in my prayers all day. God is amazing and our faith and unity will reveal His grace and mercy. God will take care of Nate.

—Gary Hawks

Though I have never had the good fortune of meeting Nate, we have a number of mutual friends, and that is how I became aware of his situation. I have been requesting prayers for Nate on my own Facebook page and we are praying for him at the church where I serve as pastor. To Nate and his family, know [that] you are loved, cared about, and prayed for by people all the way to New Jersey, and probably even farther than that. May God bless you all in this difficult time.

—Daniel B. Casselberry

GOD MOMENTS

Here is a quick summary of the miracles, coincidences, or what I like to refer to as "God moments" that transpired over the first week of Nate's accident. Most occurred within the first forty-eight hours.

CHAPTER 3

1. The first miracle was the fact that Brad, a very seasoned paramedic, attended the rodeo. He just happened to be the supervisor that day and decided to cover the rodeo himself just to make it easier for the crew. Brad had no idea that Nate would be riding in the fair that evening.

Barely any of the rodeos that I had attended thus far had an ambulance on site. During Nate's benefit, Brad informed me that not only was it unusual for an ambulance to be there, but the fact that it was an advanced life support ambulance was extremely rare. As such, Brad had all of the equipment he needed to properly treat Nate.

Many months later, when Nate and I went back to Gratiot Medical Center in Alma to meet some of the people who helped save him, the ER manager told me that Brad was probably the only paramedic experienced enough to handle Nathan's situation.

2. The fact that Nathan made it to the hospital before

he bled to death was the second miracle. I would later find out that if Nate had been detained for even ten minutes more, he probably would have died. Also, Brad told me later that Dr. Bonacci, the surgeon, just happened to be in the hospital when Nathan arrived, which was another unusual coincidence. Later, Dr. Bonacci would also tell me that the anesthesiologist's physical presence also played a crucial role in Nate's resuscitation as she was able to assist with the administering of IV fluids and blood products upon his arrival. Because Nate was so critical, it was extremely beneficial that many people were available to simultaneously monitor different aspects of Nate's condition.

3. Another miracle was that Brad did not call for Spectrum Health Aero Med at the rodeo as he normally would have. Instead, his instinct directed him to the Gratiot Medical Center. If he would have called Spectrum Health Aero Med, they would have immediately loaded Nate without assessing him in the hospital. Nate very well may have bled to death in flight.

We also found out later that the doctors at Gratiot Medical Center were concerned because the hospital had a limited amount of blood on hand. The closest blood bank to replenish the hospital's supply was in Lansing, which was about an hour's drive away. Nate's situation depleted Gratiot's supply; they ran out of blood. The decision to call for a helicopter was finally made, and it arrived just in time. Nathan needed more blood. The flight crew brought four units of the blood for the flight. They used two units before they even loaded Nate into the helicopter. They were concerned that Nate might need more than the two units left during the flight.

CHAPTER 4

1. The fact that the Alma ER facility had just started a trauma unit less than six months prior to Nate's accident was our next miracle. Although it was not yet certified, it soon

would be. Therefore, they had already acquired some trauma equipment. One piece of equipment that they especially needed was a machine that could rapidly infuse a large amount of blood into Nate's body. This machine ultimately helped save his life. Tim later recalled how he heard the emergency room team calling off the number of units of blood they infused. According to emergency room notes, they infused Nate with twelve units of packed red blood cells, five units of fresh plasma, and one five-pack of platelets.

Another interesting coincidence they communicated to us was that Gratiot Medical Center had unfrozen plasma available. Earlier in the day, they had ordered plasma for another patient. It turns out that this patient refused the plasma, thus it was ready for Nate's critical situation.

Chapter 5

1. The next notable miracle was the helicopter's availability. We found out over a year later that Spectrum Health Aero Med had already been called out for a different emergency. During the flight, someone determined that the patient no longer needed to be transferred. The pilot had actually turned the helicopter around and was headed back to Grand Rapids. The team had almost made it back to the airport when Nate's call came into dispatch. They immediately turned around and headed for Alma. Thus, eight to ten minutes were shaved off the trip since they were already in the air. If the previous call had not been cancelled, Spectrum Health Aero Med would not have had a helicopter available since their second chopper was also on a call. Nate would not have received the extra two units of blood, and he would not have had a helicopter to fly him to Grand Rapids in a timely manner.

2. Another miracle was the doctor's decision to operate in Alma. When the flight crew arrived in Alma, they expected to take over immediately. Because Nate was so unstable, they

decided to open up Nate's abdomen first to try and stabilize the internal bleeding. Meghan, one of the flight nurses, told us over a year later that this was a pretty bold move on the surgeon's part since he was not a pediatric doctor. She said many times that doctors do not feel comfortable opening up a pediatric patient, especially under those conditions. She also informed us that as she watched the surgeon place at least sixty laparotomy packs into Nate's abdomen to try to stop the bleeding, she felt he had a very, very slim chance of surviving the flight because she noticed that blood was already seeping through the packing before they had even loaded him into the helicopter.

CHAPTER 6

1. Although the remaining two units of blood were used in flight, they were just enough. It was remarkable that Nate's vitals remained stable; they did not get any worse during the flight, which was not what the flight crew had expected.

CHAPTER 8

1. Dr. Robertson's decision to send Nate to Interventional Radiology is another miracle. The situation looked so bleak; I did not think that Dr. Robertson had another option when we first met him. I actually thought he was going to tell us that Nathan did not make it when he refused to look me in the eye. During Nate's final checkup with Dr. Robertson over a year later, he told me that he felt that Nate had less than a five percent chance of surviving Saturday night. Even though the odds of Nate surviving were not in his favor, Dr. Robertson did not give up on Nate, proving life is truly precious.

CHAPTER 9

1. In the Bible, Christ said that where two or three are gathered in his name that he would be with them. I am

convinced that having so many people prayerfully storm the gates of heaven changed the outcome. Over the course of the first two weeks, we would find out churches and groups of people in twenty states and eight different countries were praying for Nathan. Although the Internet made this possible, the fact that so many people reached out so quickly was simply amazing!

CHAPTER 10

1. Dr. Fromm's swift decision to operate was yet another miracle. She was a second-year resident who made the quick decision to reduce the immediate life-threatening abdominal pressure. Dr. Fromm opened Nate's abdomen right in the SICU. It was a bold move indeed! If the outcome would have been different, she could have been reprimanded. By 8:50 p.m., Nate's blood pressure had dropped to 40s/20s, and his heart rate had decreased into the 80s. After Dr. Fromm relieved the pressure, they performed a mass blood transfusion protocol, which stabilized Nate's blood pressure so that he could be rushed to surgery.

CHAPTER 12

1. Another interesting fact was that, for the most part, Nate did not suffer from infections until later on. At one point during the first few days, the doctor told us that the only thing he had going for him was the fact that he had no infections. An infection at the wrong time could have gravely changed the outcome.

AFTERWORD

1. Almost six months after the accident, we visited Dr. Bonacci, the surgeon in Alma. He was surprised to see Nate and said he could not believe Nate was able to walk. Dr. Bonacci commented on the fact that since Nate had lost so much blood, he probably did not have much

oxygen flowing to his brain for at least ten minutes. Since brain damage could occur in as little as four minutes, Dr. Bonacci informed us that he was extremely happy to see Nate walking around and doing well.

2. Finally, approximately one hundred and fifty units of blood and blood products were needed to save Nate's life during his Gratiot Medical Center and Butterworth ICU stays. Considering he had almost four liters of blood pooled in his abdomen in Alma, and that a healthy one-hundred and fifty-pound male has approximately five liters of blood in his body, it was truly a miracle that Nathan survived!

WORKS CITED

Donovan, Colin B. "Last Rites." ewtn.com. July 18, 2001. http://www.ewtn.com/vexperts/showmessage.asp?number =342067 (accessed June 29, 2015).

Editorial Staff. "One Bread, One Body." Presentation Ministries. August 9, 2014. http://www.presentationministries. com/obob/obob.asp?d=8/9/2014 (accessed July 12, 2015).

Eternal Word Television Network (EWTN). The Holy Rosary in Sacred Scripture. n.d. https://www.ewtn.com/Devotionals/ prayers/rosary/scripture.htm (accessed April 24, 2016).

Fr. Carlos Martins, CC. "About Relics." Treasures of the Church. n.d. http://www.treasuresofthechurch.com/about-relics (accessed July 12, 2015).

Marians of the Immaculate Conception. "What is Divine Mercy? The Chaplet of The Divine Mercy." The Divine Mercy. 2015. http://thedivinemercy.org/message/devotions/ chaplethistory.php (accessed January 28, 2015).

"Matt Maher Lyrics." azlyrics.com. n.d. www.azlyrics.com/ lyrics/mattmaher/lordineedyou.html (accessed June 30 2015).

Obetts, Tiffany L. "8 seconds. 97 units." Safety Central. August 28, 2014.

United States Conference of Catholic Bishops. Psalms, Chapter 46. n.d. http://www.usccb.org/bible/psalms/46 (accessed August 15, 2016).

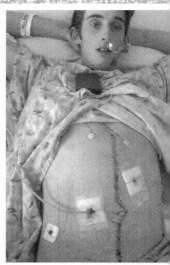

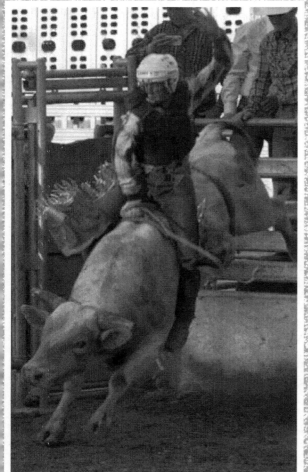

UPPER LEFT: Nathan and his fellow riders praying during opening cermemony for the Rodeo at the 2014 Clare County Fair

UPPER RIGHT: Nathan shows off his stitches at Butterworth Hospital

LOWER LEFT: Nathan riding a bull at the Clare County Fair *Photo Credit: Dottie Brugger*

LOWER RIGHT: Nathan's abdomen velcroed shut

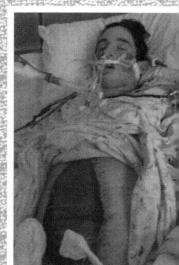

TOP: Nathan's friend and family show their support with Get Well Soon poster

RIGHT: Nathan mentally prepares for his ride at the Clare County Fair

LOWER LEFT: Nathan's medical pumps, which we famously referred to as "The Tree"

UPPER LEFT: Nathan with Father Christian Tabers from Our Lady Consolata in Sebewaing, Michigan

TOP CENTER: Nathan with Brad Doepker at benefit held in Nathan's honor in Clare, Michigan.

UPPER RIGHT: Dr. Dan Robertson and his wife Nicole posing with Nathan at the Davis family 2016 Labor Day celebration

CENTER: Nathan posing with the ER staff from Gratiot Medical Center in Alma, Michigan

LOWER LEFT: Nathan posing with Dr. Jeffrey Bonacci at his medical practice in Alma, Michigan

BOTTOM CENTER: Nathan with Rep. Joel Johnson at benefit held in Nathan's honor in Clare, Michigan.

LOWER RIGHT: Nathan and his family posing with the flight crew from Spectrum Health Aero Med

DAVIS FAMILY PHOTO

FROM LEFT TO RIGHT
Andrew, Mathew, Dani, Michelle, Tim, Nate, and Nick

ABOUT THE AUTHOR

Michelle Davis grew up in a small, rural town in Central Michigan with her parents and three brothers. She married her high school sweetheart, Tim Davis, and together they have raised five children: Danielle, Nathan, Nicholas, Mathew, and Andrew on their little hobby farm in Beaverton, Michigan, where they enjoy raising cows, pigs, and chickens.

Michelle graduated from Central Michigan University where she received a bachelor's degree in computer science. After working for almost eight years in the technology industry, she left to dedicate herself to her family. Since then, Michelle has adopted many roles: wife, mother, teacher, coach, den leader, Boy Scout mentor, and most recently, youth minister. She has a passion for teaching almost any subject but especially loves Catholic theology and mathematics.

A devout Catholic, Michelle believes that God has a plan for everyone. She tries to not only live this message every day but also help others recognize this fact too. Michelle knows how God has blessed her family and feels called to share her family's experience to bring hope to others.

75909900R00130

Made in the USA
Columbia, SC
30 August 2017